$1 -

Memorable providences, relating to witchcrafts and possesions : a faithful account of many wonderful and surprising things, that have befallen several bewitched and possessed persons in New-England ... : whereunto is added, A discourse delivered unto a...

Cotton Mather

MEMORABLE PROVIDENCES,

Relating to

VVITCHCRAFTS and POSSESSIONS:

A Faithful Account of many Wonderful and Surprising Things, that have befallen several *Bewitched* and *Possessed* Persons in *New-England*.

Particularly, a NARRATIVE of the marvellous *Trouble* and *Relief*, Experienced by a pious Family in *Boston*, very lately and sadly molested with Evil SPIRITS.

Whereunto is added,

A Discourse delivered unto a Congregation in *Boston*, on the Occasion of that *Illustrious Providence*.

As also, A Discourse delivered unto the same Congregation; on the occasion of an horrible *Self-Murder* Committed in the Town.

With an Appendix, in vindication of a Chapter in a late Book of Remarkable Providences, from the Calumnies of a Quaker at *Pen-silvania*.

Written by Cotton Mather, *Minister of the Gospel*.

And Recommended by the Ministers of *Boston* and *Charleston*.

Printed at *Boston* in *New-England*, and Re-printed at *Edinburgh* by the Heirs and Successors of *Andrew Anderson*, Printer to His most Excellent Majesty *Anno* DOM. 1697.

To the Honourable WAIT VVINTRHROP Esq;

Sr. BY the special Disposal and Providence of the Almighty God, there now comes abroad into the world, a little History of several very astonishing *Witchcrafts* and *Possessions*, which partly my own *Ocular Observation*, and partly my *undoubted Information*, hath enabled me to offer unto the publick Notice of my Neighbours. It must be the *Subject*, and not the *Manner* or the *Author* of this Writing, that has made any people desire its Publication, For there are such obvious *Defects* in *Both*, as would render me very unreasonable, if I should wish about *This* or *Any* Composure of mine, *O that it were printed in a Book*! But tho' there want not *Faults* in the Discourse, to give me Discontent enough, my Displeasure at *them* will be recompensed by the Satisfaction I take in my *Dedication* of it; which I now, no less *properly* than *cheerfully* make unto Your Self, whom I reckon among the *Best* of my *Friends*, and the *Ablest* of my *Readers*. Your *Knowledge* has *Qualified* You to make those Reflections on the following Relations, which *few* can *Think*, and 'tis not *fit* that *all* should *See*, How far the *Platonic Notions* of *Dæmons* which were, it may be, much more espoused by those *primitive* Christians and Scholars that we call *The Fathers*, than they seem countenanced in the ensuing *Narratives*, are to be allowed by a serious man, Your *Scriptural Divinity*, joyn'd with Your most *Rational Philosophy*, will help You to judge at an *uncommon* rate. Had I on the Occasion before me handled the *Doctrine of Dæmons*, or lanched forth into Speculations about *magical Mysteries*, I might have made some Ostentation, that I have *read* something and *thought* a little in my time, but it would neither have been *Convenient* for me, nor *profitable* for those *plain Folks*, whose *Edification* I have all along aimed at. I have therefore here but *briefly toucht* every thing with an *American Pen*; a Pen which your *Desert* likewise has further *Entituled* You to the utmost Expressions of Respect and Honour *from*. Though I have no *Commission*, yet I am sure I shal meet with no *Crimination*, if I here publickly *wish you all manner of Happiness*, in the Name *of the great Multitudes whom you have laid under everlasting Obligations*. Wherefore *in the name* of the many hundred *Sick* people, whom your *charitable* and *skilful* Hands have most *freely* dispensed your no less *generous* than *secret* Medicines to; and in the name of Your *whole Countrey*, which hath long had cause to believe that you will succeed Your Honourable *Father* and *Grandfather*, in successful Endeavours for our Welfare: I say, In their Name, I now do wish you all the *Prosperity* of them that love *Jerusalem*. And whereas it hath been sometimes observed, That *the Genius of an Author is commonly* Discovered in the Dedicatory Epistle, I shall be content if this *Dedicatory Epistle* of mine, have now *discovered* me to be,

(Sir) Your sincere and very humble Servant,

C. Mather.

To the Reader.

THe old Heresie of the sensual Sadducees, denying the Beeing of Angels either good or evil, died not with them; nor will it, whiles men (abandoning both Faith and Reason) count it their wisdom to credit nothing but what they see and feel. How much this fond opinion has gotten ground in this debauched Age is awfully observable; and what a dangerous stroak it gives to settle men in Atheism, is not hard to discern. God is therefore pleased (besides the witness born to this Truth in Sacred Writ) to suffer Devils sometimes to do such things in the world as shall stop the mouth of gain-sayers, and extort a Confession from them.

It has also been made a doubt by some, whether there are any such things as Witches, i. e. Such as by Contract or Explicit Covenant with the Devil, improve, or rather are improved by him to the doing of things strange in themselves, and besides their natural Course. But (besides that the Word of God assures us that there have been such, and gives order about them) no Age passes without some apparent Demonstration of it. For, Though it be folly to impute every dubious Accident, or unwonted Effect of Providence, to Witchcraft; yet there are some things which cannot be excepted against, but must be ascribed hitherto.

Angels and Men not being made for a civil Converse together in this world, and all Communion with Devils being interdicted us, their Nature also being Spiritual, and the Word of God having said so little in that particular concerning their way of Acting, hence it is that we can disclose but a little of those Mysteries of Darkness, all reports that are from themselves, or their Instruments, being to be esteemed as Illusions, or at least covered with Deceit, filled with the Impostures of the Father of Lies, and the effects which come under our consideration being Mysterious, rather Posing than Informing us.

The Secrets also of God's Providence, in permitting Satan and his Instruments to molest His Children, not in their Estates only, but in their Persons and their Posterity too, are part of His Judgments that are unsearchable, and His Ways that are past finding out, only this we have good Assurance for, that they are among the All things that work together for their good. Their Graces are hereby tried, their Uprightness is made known, their Faith and Patience have their perfect work.

Among the many Instances that have been of this kind, That which is Recorded in this Narrative, is worthy to be commended to the Notice of Mankind. It being a thing in it self full of Memorable Passages, and faithfully Recorded according to the Truth in Matter of Fact, scarce any Instance being asserted in it, but what hath the Evi-

dence

dence of many credible Witnesses, did need require. Among others who had frequent Occasions to observe these things, the Reverend Author of this short History, was spirited to be more than ordinarily engaged in attending, and making particular Remarks upon the several Passages occurring therein; and hath accordingly written very little besides what himself was an Eye-witness of, together with others, and the rest was gathered up with much Accuracy and Caution.

It is needless for us to insist upon the Commendation either of the Author or the Work, the former is known in the Churches, the latter will speak sufficiently for it self. All that we shall offer to stay the Reader from passing over to satisfie himself in that which follows, is only thus much, Viz. That the following Account will afford to him that shall read with Observation a further clear Confirmation, That, There is both a GOD, and a Devil, and Witchcraft. *That,* There is no outward Affliction, but what God may (and sometimes doth) permit Satan to trouble His People withal. *That,* The Malice of Satan and his Instruments, is very great against the Children of God. *That,* The clearest Gospel-Light shining in a place, will not keep some from entring Hellish Contracts with Infernal Spirits. *That,* Prayer is a powerful and effectual Remedy against the Malicious Practices of Devils, and those in Covenant with them. *That,* They who will obtain such Mercies of God, must pray unto Perseverance: *That,* God often gives to His People some apparent encouragements to their Faith in Prayer, though He does not presently perfect the Deliverance sought for. *That,* God's Grace is able to support His Children, and preserve their Grace firm, under sorest and Continuing Troubles. *That,* Those who refuse the Temptation to use Doubtful or Diabolical Courses, to get the Assaults of the Devil and his Agents removed, Choosing to Recommend all to God, and rather to endure Affliction, than to have it removed to His *Dishonour* and the wounding of their own Consciences, never had cause to repent of it in the end.

And if these Observations, together with the solemn Improvement made of this stupend Providence, in the pertinent and Judicious Sermons annexed, may but obtain a due Impression on the hearts of such as shall peruse them, whether young or old, as therein will be their profit, so shall their Labour therein to the Praise of God fully satisfie the Author for all his Care and Industry, and answer his sincere Aims: for which good Success we Commend it to the Blessing of God, to be followed with the importunate Prayers of us, who have been Eye and Ear-witnesses of many of the most considerable things Related in the ensuing Narrative.

Charles Morton.

James Allen.

Joshua Moodey.

Samuel Willard.

The Introduction.

IT was once the miſtake of one gone to the *Congregation of the Dead* concerning the Survivers, *If one went unto them from the dead, they will repent.* The bleſſed God hath made ſome to *come from the Damned,* for the *Conviction* (may it alſo be for the *Converſion*) of us that are yet alive. The *Devils* themſelves are by Compulſion come to confute the *Atheiſm* and *Sadduciſm*, and to reprove the madneſs of *ungodly men.* Thoſe condemned priſoners of our *Atmoſphere* have not really ſent *Letters of Thanks* from *Hell*, to thoſe that are on *Earth*, promoting of their Intereſt; yet they have been forced, as of old, *To confeſs that Jeſus was the Holy One of God*, ſo of late, *to declare that Sin and Vice are the things which they are delighted in.* But should one of thoſe hideous *Wights* appear viſibly with fiery chains upon him, and utter audibly his Roarings and his Wailings in one of our *Congregations*, it would not produce new *Hearts* in thoſe whom the *Scripture* handled in our *Miniſtry* do not affect. However it becomes the *Embaſſadors of the Lord Jeſus* to leave no ſtroke untouch'd that may conduce to bring men from the power of *Satan* unto *God*; and for this cauſe it is, that I have permitted the enſuing *Hiſtories* to be publiſhed. They contain Things of undoubted Certainty, and they ſuggeſt Things of Importance unconceivable. Indeed they are only one Head of Collections which in my little time of Obſervation I have made of Memorable Providences, with Reflections thereupon to be reſerved among other effects of my Diverſion from my more ſtated and more weary Studies. But I can with a Contentment beyond meer Patience, give theſe reſcinded Sheets unto the Stationer, when I ſee what pains Mr. *Baxter*, Mr. *Glanvil*, Dr. *More*, and ſeveral other great Names have taken to publiſh Hiſtories of *Witchcrafts* and *Poſſeſſions* unto the world. I ſaid, Let me alſo run after them; and this with the more *Alacrity*, becauſe I have tidings ready. Go then my little Book, as a Lackey to the more elaborate Eſſayes of thoſe learned men. Go tell Mankind, that there are *Devils* and *Witches*, and that tho' thoſe *night-birds* leaſt appear where the *Day-light* of the Goſpel comes, yet *New-England* has had Examples of their Exiſtence and Operation, and that not only the *Wigwams* of *Indians*, where the Pagan *Powaws* often raiſe their maſters, in the ſhapes of *Bears*, and *Snakes* and *Fires*, but the Houſes of Chriſtians, where our God has had His conſtant *Worſhip*, have undergone the Annoyance of Evil *Spirits.* Go tell the world, what Prayers can do beyond all *Devils* and *Witches*, and what it is that theſe *Monſters* love to do, and though the *Dæmons* in the Audience of ſeveral ſtanders-by threatned much *Diſgrace* to thy Author, if he let thee come abroad, yet venture That, and in this way ſeek a juſt Revenge on Them for the Diſturbance they have given to ſuch as *have called on the Name of* GOD.

Witchcrafts and *Possessions.*

The *First* EXAMPLE.

§. 1. THere dwells at this time, in the South part of *Boston*, a sober and pious man, whose Name is *John Goodwin*, whose Trade is that of a Mason, and whose Wife (to which a Good Report gives a share with him in all the Characters of Vertue) has made him the Father of six (now living) Children. Of these Children, all but the Eldest, who works with his Father at his Calling, and the Youngest, who lives yet upon the Breast of its Mother, have laboured under the direful effects of a (no less palpable than) stupendious *WITCHCRAFT*. Indeed that exempted Son had also, as was thought, some lighter Touches of it, in unaccountable Stabbs and Pains now and then upon him; as indeed every person in the Family at some time or other had, except the Godly Father, and the Sucking Infant, who never felt any Impressions of it. But these four Children mentioned, were handled in so sad and strange a manner, as has given matter of Discourse and Wonder to all the Countrey, and of History not unworthy to be considered by more than all the serious or the curious Readers in this *New-English* World.

§. 2. The four Children (whereof the Eldest was about Thirteen, and the Youngest was perhaps about a third part so many Years of Age) had enjoy'd a Religious Education, and answered it with a very towardly Ingenuity. They had an observable Affection unto Divine and Sacred things; and those of them that were capable of it, seem'd to have such a Resentment of their Eternal Concernments, as is not altogether usual. Their

Parents alſo kept them to a continual Employmen which did more than deliver them from the Temptat ons of Idleneſs, and as young as they were, they too a delight in it, it may be as much as they ſhould hav done. In a word, Such was the whole Temper an Carriage of the Children, that there cannot eaſily b any thing more unreaſonable, than to imagine that Deſign to Diſſemble could cauſe them to fall into an of their odd Fits; though there ſhould not have hap pened, as there did, a thouſand Things, wherein was perfectly impoſſible for any Diſſimulation of thei to produce what Scores of Spectators were amazed at.

§. 3. About *Midſummer*, in the year 1688, the E deſt of theſe Children, who is a Daughter, ſaw cauſe examine their Waſher-woman, upon their miſſing ſome Linnen, which 'twas fear'd ſhe had ſtollen fro them; and of what uſe this Linnen might be to ſer the Witchcraft intended, the Theef's Tempter know This Laundreſs was the Daughter of an Ignorant and Scandalous old Woman in the Neighbourhood; who miſerable Husband before he died, had ſometimes con plained of her, that ſhe was undoubtedly a Witch, an that whenever his Head was laid, ſhe would quickly a rive unto the puniſhments due to ſuch a one. This W man in her Daughters Defence beſtow'd very bad La guage upon the Girl that put her to the Queſtion; imm diatly upon which, the poor Child became variouſly i diſpoſed in her health, and viſited with ſtrange Fi beyond thoſe that attend an *Epilepſy*, or a *Catalepſy*, thoſe that they call *The Diſeaſes of Aſtoniſhment*.

§. 4. It was not long before one of her Siſters, an two of her Brothers, were ſeized, in Order one aft another, with Affects like thoſe that moleſted he Within a few Weeks, they were all four tortured ev ry where in a manner ſo very grievous, that it wou have broke an heart of ſtone to have ſeen their Ag nies. Skilful Phyſicians were conſulted for their Hel and particularly our Worthy and Prudent Friend D

Ch

tor *Thomas Oakes*, who found himself so affronted by Distempers of the Children, that he concluded no-hing but an Hellish Witchcraft could be the Original f these Maladies. And that which yet more confirmed ich Apprehension was, That for one good while, the hildren were tormented just in the same part of their odies all at the same time together; and though they w and heard not one anothers Complaints, though kewise their Pains and Sprains were swift like Lighte-ing, yet when (suppose) the Neck, or the Hand, or heBack of one was Rackt, so it was at that Instant vith the other too.

§. 5. The variety of their Tortures increased con-inually; and though about Nine or Ten at Night they lways had a Release from their miseries, and ate and lept all night for the most part indifferently well, yet n the day time they were handled with so many sorts of Ails, that it would require of us almost as much time o Relate them all, as it did of them to Endure them. ometimes they would be Deaf, sometimes Dumb, and ometimes Blind, and often, all this at once. One while their Tongues would be drawn down their Throats, nother while they would be pull'd out upon their Chins, o a prodigious length. They would have their Mouths pened unto such a Wideness, that their Jaws went out of joynt; and anon they would clap together again vith a Force like that of a strong Spring-Lock. The ame would happen to their Shoulder Blades, and their Elbows, and Hand-wrists, and several of their joints. They vould at times ly in a benummed condition, & be drawn ogether as those that are ty'd Neck and Heels; and presently be stretched out, yea, drawn backwards, to ich a degree that it was fear'd the very skin of their Bellies would have cracked. They would make most piteous out-cries, that they were cut with Knives, and truck with Blows that they could not bear. Their Necks would be broken, so that their Neck-bone would eem dissolved unto them that felt after it; and yet on

 the

the sudden, it would become again so stiff that there was no stirring of their Heads; yea, their Heads would be twisted almost round; and if main Force at any time obstructed a dangerous motion which they seem'd to be upon, they would roar exceedingly. Thus they lay some Weeks most pitiful Spectacles; and this while as a further Demonstration of Witchcraft in these horrid Effects, when I went to Prayer by one of them, that was very desirous to hear what I said, the Child utterly lost her Hearing till our Prayer was over.

§. 6. It was a Religious Family that these Afflictions happened unto; and none but a Religious Contrivance to obtain Relief, would have been welcome to them. Many superstitious Proposals were made unto them, by persons that were I know not who, nor what, with Arguments fetcht from I know not how much Necessity and Experience; but the distressed Parents rejected all such counsels, with a gracious Resolution, to oppose Devils with no other Weapons but Prayers and Tears unto Him that has the Chaining of them; and to try first whether Graces were not the best things to encounter Witchcrafts with. Accordingly they requested the four Ministers of *Boston*, with the Minister of *Charlstown* to keep a Day of Prayer at their thus Haunted House; which they did in the Company of some Devout People there. Immediatly upon this Day, the Youngest of the four Children was delivered, and never felt any trouble as afore. But there was yet a greater Effect of these our Applications unto our GOD!

§. 7. The Report of the Calamities of the Family for which we were thus concerned, arrived now unto the Ears of the Magistrats, who presently and prudently apply'd themselves, with a just vigour, to enquire into the Story. The Father of the Children complained of his Neighbour, the suspected ill Woman, whose Name was *Glover*; and she being sent for by the Justices, gave such a wretched Account of her self, that they saw cause to commit her unto the Gaolers Custody. *Good*-

win had no proof that could have done her any Hurt; but the Hag had not power to deny her intereſt in the Enchantment of the Children; and when ſhe was asked, *Whether ſhe believed there was a God?* her Anſwer was too blaſphemous and horrible for any Pen of mine to mention. An Experiment was made, Whether ſhe could recite the Lords Prayer; and it was found, that though clauſe after Clauſe was moſt carefully repeated unto her, yet when ſhe ſaid it after them that prompted her, ſhe could not poſſibly avoid making Nonſenſe of it, with ſome ridiculous Depravations. This Experiment I had the curioſity ſince to ſee made upon two more, & it had the ſame Event. Upon the Commitment of this extraordinary Woman, all the Children had ſome preſent eaſe; until one (related unto her) accidentally meeting one or two of them, etertain'd them with her Bleſſing, that is, Railing; upon which three of them fell ill again, as they were before.

§. 8. It was not long before the Witch thus in the Trap, was brought upon her Tryal; at which, thro' the Efficacy of a Charm, I ſuppoſe, uſed upon her by one or ſome of her Crew, the Court could receive Anſwers from her in none but the *Iriſh*, which was her Native Language; although ſhe underſtood the *Engliſh* very well, and had accuſtomed her whole Family to none but that Language in her former Converſation; and therefore the Communication between the Bench and the Bar, was now chiefly convey'd by two honeſt and faithful men that were Interpreters. It was long before ſhe could with any direct Anſwers plead unto her Indictment; and when ſhe did plead, it was with Confeſſion rather than Denial of her Guilt. Order was given to ſearch the old Womans Houſe, from whence there were brought into the Court, ſeveral ſmall Images, or Puppets, or Babies, made of Raggs, and ſtuff't with Goats hair, and other ſuch Ingredients. When theſe were produced, the vile Woman acknowledged, that her way to torment the Objects of her Malice, was

by,

by wetting of her Finger with her Spittle, and stroaking of those little Images. The abused Children were then present, and the Woman still kept stooping and shrinking as one that was almost prest to Death with a mighty Weight upon her. But one of the Images being brought unto her, immediatly she started up after an odd manner, and took it into her Hand; but she had no sooner taken it, than one of the Children fell into sad fits, before the whole Assembly. This the Judges had their just Apprehensions at; & carefully causing the Repetition of the Experiment, found again the same event of it. They asked her whether she had any to stand by her: She replied, she had; and looking very pertly in the Air, she added, No, he's gone. And she then confessed, that she had one who was her Prince, with whom she maintained, I know not what Communion. [illegible] which cause the night after, she was heard expostulating with a *Devil*, for his thus deserting her; telling him that, because he had served her so basely and falsly she had confessed all. However to make all clear, The Court appointed five or six *Physicians*, one evening to examine her very strictly, whether she were not craz'd in her Intellectuals, and had not procured to her self by Folly and Madness the Reputation of a *Witch*. Diverse Hours did they spend with her; and in all that while no Discourse came from her, but what was pertinent and agreeable: particularly, when they asked her, What she thought would become of her soul? she replied, *You ask me a very solemn Question, and I cannot well tell what to say to it.* She own'd her self a *Roman Catholick*, and could recite her *Pater Noster* in Latine very readily; but there was one Clause or two always too hard for her, whereof she said, *She could not repeat it, if she might have all the world.* In the up-shot, the Doctors returned her *Compos Mentis* and Sentence of Death was pass'd upon her.

§. 9. Diverse days were passed between her being *Arraigned* and *Condemned*. In this time one of her Neighbours

urs had been giving in her Testimony of what another of her Neighbours had upon her Death related concerning her. It seems one *Howen* about Six years before, had been cruelly bewitched to Death; but before she died, she called one *Hughs* unto her, Telling her that she laid her Death to the charge of *Glover*; That she had seen *Glover* sometimes come down her Chimney; That she should remember *this*, for within Six years she might have Occasion to declare it. This *Hughs* now preparing her Testimony, immediatly one of her Children, a fine Boy, well grown towards Youth, was taken ill, just in the same woful and surprising manner that *Goodwins* children were. One night particularly, The Boy said he saw a Black thing with a Blue Cap in the Room, tormenting of him; and he complained most bitterly of a Hand put into the Bed, to pull out his Bowels. The next day the mother of the Boy went unto *Glover*, in the Prison, & asked her, Why she tortured her poor lad at such a wicked rate? This Witch replied, that she did it because of wrong done to her self and her daughter. *Hughs* denied (as well she might) that she had done her any wrong. Well then, says *Glover*, Let me see your child and he shal be well again. *Glover* went on, and told her of her own accord, I was at your House last night. Says *Hughs*, in what shape? Says *Glover*, As a black thing with a blue Cap. Says *Hughs*, What did you do there? Says *Glover*, with my Hand in the Bed I tryed to pull out the Boyes Bowels, but I could not. They parted; but the next day *Hughs* appearing at Court, had her Boy with her; and *Glover* passing by the Boy, expressed her good wishes for him; tho' I suppose, his Parent had no design of any mighty Respect unto the *Hag*, by having him with her there. But the Boy had no more Indispositions after the Condemnation of the Woman.

§ 9 While the miserable old Woman was under Condemnation, I did my self twice give a visit unto her. She never denied the guilt of the *Witchcraft* charg'd upon her

her; but she confessed very little about the Circumstanc of her Confedracy with the *Devils*; only, she said, th she us'd to be ot meetings, which her Prince and Fo more were present at. As for those Four, She told wh they were; and for her Prince, her account plain was, that he was the *Devil*. She entertained me wi nothing but *Irish*, which Language I had not learning nough to understand without an Interpreter; only o time, when I was representing unto her that and ho her Prince had cheated her, as her self would quick find; she reply'd, I think in *English*, and with passi too. If it be so, I am sorry for that! I offered man Questions unto her, unto which, after long silence, s told me, She would fain give me a full Answer, but th would not give her leave. It was demanded, *They Who is that* THEY? and she returned, that They we her Spirits, or her Saints. [for they say the same Wo in *Irish* signifies both] And at another time, she inclu ed her two Mistresses, as she call'd them in that [They but when it was enquired, who these two were, s fell into a Rage, and would be no more urged.

I set before her, the Necessity and Equity of her brea ing her Covenant with *Hell*, and giving her self to th Lord Jesus Christ, by an everlasting Covenant; T which her Answer was, that I spake a very reasonab thing, but she could not do it. I asked her whether s would consent or desire to be pray'd for; To that s said, If Prayer would do her any good, she could pr for her self. And when it was again propounded, s said, She could not unless her spirits [or angels] wou give her leave However, against her will I pray'd wi her, which if it were a Fault it was in excess of Pit When I had done, she thanked me with many go Words; but I was no sooner out of her sight, than s took a Stone, a long & slender Stone, and with her Fi ger & Spittle fell to tormenting it; though whom or wh she meant, I had the mercy never to understand.

§. 11. When this *Witch* was going to her Executio

e said, the Children should not be relieved by Death, r others had a hand in it as well as She; and she named e among the rest, whom it might have been thought tural -ffection would have advised the Concealing of. came to pass accordingly, That the three Children ntinued in their Furnace as before, and it grew raer seven times hotter than it was. All their former ils pursued them still, with an addition of ('tis not sie to tell how many) more, but such as gave more nsible Demonstrations of an Enchantment growing vey far towards a *Possession* by evil Spirits.

§. 12. The Children in their Fits would still cry out pon [They] and [Them] as the Authors of all heir Harm ; but who that [They] and [Them were] hey were not able to declare At last, the Boy obtaind at some times, a sight of some shapes in the Room. There were three or four of 'em, the names of which the Child would pretend at certain seasons to tell ; only the ame of one, who was counted a *Sager Hag* than the est, he still so stammered at, that he was put upon some *Periphrasis* in describing her. A Blow at the place where the Boy beheld the Spectre was always felt by the Boy himself in the part of his Body that answered what might be stricken at ; and this tho' his Back were turn'd; which was once and again so exactly tried, that there could be no Collusion in the Business. But as a Blow at the Apparition always hurt him, so it always help't him too ; for after the Agonies, which a Push or Stab of that had put him to, were over, (as in a minut or 2 they would be) the Boy would have a respite from his Fits a considerable while, and the Hobgoblins disappear. It is very credibly reported that a wound was this way given to an Ohnoxious Woman in the Town ; whose name I will not expose: for we should be tender in such Relations, lest we wrong the Reputation of the Innocent, by stories not enough enquired into.

§. 13. The Fits of the Children yet more arriv'd unto such Motions as were beyond the Efficacy of any natural

tural

ural Distemper in the world. They would bark at o another like Dogs, and again purr like so many Ca They would sometimes complain that they were ir Red-hot Oven, sweating and panting at the same tir unreasonably: Anon they would say, Cold water w thrown upon them, at which they would shiver ve much. They would cry out of dismal Blows with gre Cudgels laid upon them; and tho' we saw no Cudg nor Blows, yet we could see the Marks left by them Red Strakes upon their Bodies afterward. And one them would be roasted on an invisible Spit, run into h Mouth, and out at his Foot, he lying and rolling, ar groaning as if he had been so in the most sensible ma ner in the world; and then he would shriek, that Kniv were cutting of him. Sometimes also he would ha his head so forcibly, tho not visibly nail'd unto the Flo that it was as much as a strong man could do to pull up. One while they they would *all* be so Limber, th it was judg'd every Bone of them could be bent. An ther while they would be so stiff, that not a Joint them could be stirr'd. They would sometimes be though they were mad, and then they would climb ov high Fences, beyond the Imagination of them that loo after them. Yea, they would fly like Geese; and l carried with an incredible Swiftness thro the Air, havin but just their Toes now and then upon the ground, ar their Arms waved like the Wings of a Bird. One them, in the House of a kind Neighbour and Gentlema (Mr. *Willis*) flew the length of the Room, about Foot, and flew just into an Infants high armed Chair (as 'tis affirmed) none seeing her Feet all the w touch the Floor.

§. 14. Many ways did the *Devils* take to make th Children do mischief both to themselves and others; b through the singular Providence of God, they alwa fail'd in the attempts. For they could never essay th doing of any harm, unless there were some body hand that might prevent it; and seldome without fi

shrieki

rieking out, *They say, I must do such a thing!* Diverse nes they went to strike furious Blows at their tender- [and dearest Friends, or to fling them down stairs jen they had them at the Top, but the warnings from e mouths of the Children themselves, would still an- cipate what the Devils did intend. They diverse times ere very near Burning or Drowning of themselves, but e Children themselves by their own pitiful and season- le cryes for help, still procured their Deliverance: Vhich made me to consider, whether the little Ones id not their Angels, in the plain sense of our Saviours timation. Sometimes, when they were tying their vn Neck-clothes, their compelled hands miserably rangled themselves, till perhaps, the standers by gave me Relief unto them. But if any small mischief hap- ed to be done, where they were, as the tearing or dir- ing of a Garment; the falling of a Cup, the breaking f a Glass, or the like; they would rejoyce extreamly id fall into a pleasure or laughter very extraordinary. ll which things compared with the temper of the chil- ren, when they are themselves, may suggest some very eculiar thoughts unto us.

§. 15. They were not in a constant torture for some Veeks, but were a little quiet, unless upon some inci- ental provocations; upon which the *Devils* would handle iem like Tigres, and wound them in a manner very orribly. Particularly, upon the least Reproof of their arents for any unfit thing they said or did, most griev- us woful heart-breaking Agonies would they fall into. any useful thing were to be done to them, or by them, ey would have all sorts of troubles fall upon them. It ould sometimes cost one of them an hour or two to be idrest in the evening, or drest in the morning. For if e went to unty a string, or undo a Button about them, the contrary; they would be twisted into such post- es as made the thing impossible. And at whiles, they ould be so managed in their Beds, that no Bed-clothes ould for an hour or two be laid upon them; nor could

they

they go to wash their Hands, without having them cla
so odly together, there was no doing of it. But w
their Friends were near tired with Waiting, anon t
might do what they would unto them. Whatever w
they were bid to do, they would be so snap't in the me
ber which was to do it, that they with grief stil de
ed from it. If one ordered them to rub a clean Ta
they were able to do it without any disturbance; if
rub a dirty Table, presently they would with many t
ments be made uncapable. And sometimes, tho
seldome, they were kept from eating their meals,
having their Teeth set, when they carried any th
unto their Mouths.

§. 16. But nothing in the world would so disco
pose them as a Religious Exercise. If there were a
discourse of God, or Christ, or any of the things wh
are not seen and are eternal, they would be cast into
tollerable *Anguishes*. Once, those two worthy Mi
sters Mr. *Fisk* and Mr. *Thatcher*, bestowing some gra
ous Counsels on the Boy, whom they then found at
Neighbours house, he immediatly lost his Hearing,
that he heard not one word, but just the last word of
they said. Much more, All Praying to God, and readi
of his Word, would occasion a very terrible vexati
to them: they would then stop their own Ears wi
their own Hands; and roar, and shriek, and holla,
drown the Voice of the Devotion. Yea, if any one
the Room took up a Bible to look into it, tho the Ch
dren could see nothing of it, as being in a croud of Sp
ctators, or having their Faces another way, yet wou
they be in wonderful Miseries, till the Bible were la
aside. In short, No good thing must then be endur
near those Children, Which (while they are the
selves) do love every good thing in a measure th
proclaims in them the fear of God.

§. 17 My Employments were such, that I could n
visit this afflicted Family so often as I would; Whe
fore that I might show them what kindness I could,

all

ſo that I might have a full Opportunity to obſerve the
ꝏtraordinary Circumſtances of the Children, and that
might be furniſhed with Evidence and Argument as a
ritical Eye-Witneſs to confute the Saduciſm of this
ebauched Age; I took the Eldeſt of them home to my
ouſe The young Woman continued well at our houſe
or diverſe days, and applyed her ſelf to ſuch Actions
ot only of Induſtry, but of Piety, as ſhe had been no
ranger to. But on the twentieth of *November* in the
ore-noon, ſhe cryed out, *Ah, They have found me out! thought it would be ſo!* and immediatly ſhe fell into her
ts again. I ſhal now confine my Story chiefly to Her,
om whoſe Caſe the Reader may ſhape ſome Conjecture
: the Accidents of the Reſt.

§. 18. Variety of Tortures now ſeiz'd upon the Girl;
n which beſides the fore-mentioned Ails returning up-
n her, ſhe often would cough up a Ball as big as a
mall Egg, into the ſide of her Wind-pipe, that would
ear chook her, till by Stroking and by *Drinking* it was
arried down again. At the beginning of her Fits uſu-
lly ſhe kept odly looking up the Chimney, but could
ot ſay what ſhe ſaw. When I bade her Cry to the
Lord Jeſus for Help, her Teeth were inſtantly ſet; up
n which I added, Yet, Child, Look unto Him, and
hen her Eyes were preſently pulled into her head, ſo
ır, that one might have fear'd ſhe ſhould never have
ſ'd them more. When I prayed in the Room, firſt
er Arms were with a ſtrong, though not ſeen Force
lapt upon her Ears; and when her hands were with
iolence pull'd away, ſhe cryed out, [They] make
ıch a noiſe, I cannot hear a word! She likewiſe com-
lain'd, that Goodly *Glover's* Chain was upon her Leg,
nd when ſhe eſſay'd to go, her Poſtures were exactly
ıch as the Chained Witch had before ſhe died. But
e manner ſtill was, that her Tortures in a ſmall while
ould paſs over, and Frolicks ſucceed; in which ſhe
ould continue many hours, nay, whole days, talking
erhaps never wickedly, but always wittily beyond her
ſelf;

ſelf; and at certain provocations, her Tortures wou[ld] renew upon her, till we had left off to give them. B[ut] ſhe frequently told us, that if ſhe might but ſteal, o[r] be drunk, ſhe ſhould be well immediatly.

§. 19. In her ludicrous Fits, one while ſhe would b[e] for Flying; and ſhe would be carried hither and th[i]ther, though not long from the ground, yet ſo long a[s] to exceed the ordinary power of Nature, in our Opin[i]on of it: another while ſhe would be for Diving, an[d] uſe the Actions of it towards the Floor, on which, [if] we had not held her, ſhe would have thrown her ſel[f.] Being at this exerciſe ſhe told us, That they ſaid, ſh[e] muſt go down to the Bottom of our Well, for ther[e] was Plate there, and they ſaid, They would bring he[r] ſafely up again. This did ſhe tell us, though ſhe ha[d] never heard of any Plate there! and we our ſelves wh[o] had newly bought the houſe, hardly knew of any; bu[t] the former Owner of the houſe juſt then coming in told us there had been Plate for many years at the Bo[t]tom of the Well.

She had once a great mind to have eaten a roaſte[d] Apple, but whenever ſhe attempted to eat it, her Teet[h] would be ſet, and ſometimes, if ſhe went to take i[t] up, her Arm would be made ſo ſtiff, that ſhe coul[d] not poſſibly bring her hand to her Mouth: at laſt ſh[e] ſaid, Now they ſay, I ſhall eat it, if I eat it quickly; and ſhe nimbly eat it all up. Moreover,

There was one very ſingular Paſſion that frequentl[y] attended her. An Inviſible Chain would be clapt a-bout her, and ſhe, in much Pain and Fear, cry out When [they] began to put it on. Once I did wit[h] with my own hand knock it off, as it began to be faſt-ned about her. But ordinarily, When it was on, ſhe'd be pull'd out of her ſeat with ſuch violence toward th[e] Fire, that it has been as much as one or two of us coul[d] do to keep her out. Her Eyes were not brought to b[e] perpendicular to her Feet, when ſhe roſe out of he[r] Seat, as the Mechaniſm of a Humane Body requires i[n]

them

hem that rise, but she was one dragg'd wholly by other ands: and once, When I gave a stamp on the Hearth, ust between her and the Fire, she scream'd out, (tho think she saw me not) that I Jarr'd the Chain, and urt her Back.

§. 20. While she was in her Frolicks I was willing o try, Whether she could read or no; and I found, ot only, That if she went to read the Bible, her Eyes would be strangely twisted and blinded, and her Neck resently broken, but also that if any one else did read he Bible in the Room, though it were wholly out of er sight, and without the least voice or noise of it, he would be cast Into very terrible Agonies. Yet nce, Falling into her Maladies a little time after she ad read the 59th Psalm, I said unto the standers by, Poor Child! she can't now read the Psalm she read a while ago, she listened her self unto something that one of us could hear, and made us be silent for some ew Seconds of a Minut. Whereupon she said, But I an read it, they say I shall! So I show'd her the Psalm, and she read it all over to us. Then said I, Child, say *Amen* to it: but that she could not do. I dded, Read the next: but no where else in the Bible ould she read a word. I brought her a *Quakers* Book; nd that she could quietly read whole pages of; only he Name of GOD and CHRIST she still skipt over, beng unable to pronunce it, except sometimes with tammering a Minut or two or more upon it. When we urged her to tell what the word was that she missed, he'd say, I must not speak it; They say I must not, ou know what it is, it's G and O and D; so she'd spell he Name unto us. I brought her again, one that I hought was a good Book; and presently she was hanlledwith intolerable Torments. But when I show'd er a Jest Book, as, The *Oxford* Jests, or the *Cambrige* ests, she could read them without any Disturbance, nd have witty Descants upon them too. I entertain'd er with a Book that pretends to prove, That there are

no

no Witches; and that ſhe could read very well, o the Name Devils, and Witches, could not be uttered her without extraordinary Difficulty. I produced Book to her that proves, That there are Witches, a that ſhe had not power to read. When I read in t Room, the Story of *Ann Cole*, in my Fathers Remarka Providences, and came to the Exclamation which t Narrative ſays the *Dæmons* made upon her, [*Ah ſhe ru to the Rock!*] it caſt her into inexpreſſible Agonie and ſhe'd fall into them whenever I had the Expreſſi of, *Running to the Rock*, afterwards. A *Popiſh* Bo alſo ſhe could endure very well; but it would kill h to look into any Book, that (in my Opinion) it mig have been profitable and edifying for her to be readi of. Theſe Experimenss were often enough repeate and ſtill with the ſame Succeſs, before Witneſſes no few: The good Books that were found ſo mortal to h were chiefly ſuch as lay ever at hand in the Roo One was the *Guide to Heaven from the Word*, which I h given her. Another of them was Mr. *Willard*'s litt (but precious) Treatiſe of *Juſtification* Diverſe Boo publiſhed by my Father I alſo tried upon her; partic larly, his *Myſtery of Chriſt*; and another ſmall Book his about *Faith* and *Repentance*, and *the day of Judgmen*

Once being very merrily talking by a Table that h this laſt Book upon it, ſhe juſt opened the Book, an was immediatly ſtruck backwards as dead upon the floo I hope I have not ſpoil'd the credit of the Books, b telling how much the Devils hated them. I ſhall ther fore add, That my Grand-Father *Cottons* Cathechiſ called *Milk for Babes*, and *the Aſſemblies Catechiſm*, wou bring hideous Convulſions on the Child if ſhe lookt i to them; though ſhe had once learn't them with all t love that could be.

§. 21. I was not unſenſible that this Girls Capaci or Incapacity to read, was no Teſt for Truth to be d termin'd by, and therefore I did not proceed much fu ther in this fancyful Buſineſs, not knowing what ſnar

th

he Devils might lay for us in the Trials. A few further Trials, I confess, I did make; but what the event f 'em was, I shal not relate, because I would not offend. But that which most made me to wonder was, That one bringing to her a certain Prayer-*Book*, she not nly could read it very well, but also did read a great part f it over, and calling it her *Bible*, she took in it a delight, and put on it a Respect more than Ordinary. If he were going into her *Tortures*, at the offer of this *Book*, he would come out of her Fits and read; and her Attendants were almost under a Temptation to use it as a Charm, to make and keep her quiet. Only, when she came to the Lords Prayer, (now and then occurring in this *Book*) she would have her Eyes put out, so that she must turn over a new leaf, and then she could read again. Whereas also there are Scriptures in that *Book*, he could read them there, but if I show'd her the very same Scriptures in the *Bible*, she should sooner die than read them. And she was likewise made unable to read the Psalms in an ancient metre, which this Prayer-book had in the same volumn with it. There were, I think I may say, no less than Multitudes of Witnesses, to this odd thing; and I should not have been a faithful and honest Historian, if I had withheld from the World this part of my History: *But* I make no Reflections on it. Those inconsiderable men that are provocked at it (if any shall be of so little Sense as to be provocked) must be angry at the Devils, and not at me; their Malice, and not my Writing, deserves the *Blame* of any Aspersion which a true History, may seem to cast on a *Book* that some have enough manifested their Concerment for.

§. 22. There was another most unaccountable Circumstance which now attended her; and until she came to our House, I think she never had Experience of it. Ever now and then, an Invisible Horse would be brought unto her, by those whom she only called, them,, and, her Company: upon the Approach of which, her eyes would

would be ſtill cloſed up; for (ſaid ſhe) they ſay, I am a Tell-Tale, and therefore they will not let me ſee them. Upon this ſhe would give a Spring as one mounting a Horſe, and Settling her ſelf in a Riding-Poſture, ſhe would in her Chair be agitated as one ſometimes Ambling, ſometimes Trotting, and ſometimes Galloping very furiouſly. In theſe motions we could not perceive that ſhe was ſtirred by the ſtreſs of her feet, upon the ground; for often ſhe toucht it not; but ſhe moſtly continued in her Chair, though ſometimes in her hard Trott we doubted ſhe would have been toſſed over the Back of it. Once being angry at his Dullneſs, when ſhe ſaid, ſhe would cut off his head if ſhe had a knife, I gave her my Sheath, wherewith ſhe ſuddenly gave her ſelf a ſtroke on the Neck, but complain'd, it would not cut. When ſhe had rode a Minut or two or three, ſhe'd pretend to be at a Rendezvous with them, that were her Company; there ſhe'd maintain a Diſcourſe with them, and asking many Queſtions concerning her ſelf, (for we gave her none of ours) ſhe'd Liſten much, and Received Anſwers from them that indeed none but her ſelf perceived. Then would ſhe return and inform us, how [they] did intend to handle her for a day or two afterwards, beſides ſome other things that ſhe inquired of them. Her Horſe would ſometimes throw her, with much Violence; but ſhe would mount again; and one of the Standers-by once imagining [them] that were her Company, to be before her (for ſhe call'd unto them to ſtay for her) he ſtruck with his Cane in the Air where he thought they were, and though her eyes were wholly ſhut, yet ſhe cry'd out, that he ſtruck her. Her Fantaſtick Journeys were moſtly performed in her Chair without removing from it; but ſometimes would ſhe ride from her Chair, and be carried odly on the Floor from one part of the Room to another, in the Poſtures of a Riding Woman. If any of us asked her Who her Company were? She generally replyed, I don't know. But if we were inſtant in our Deman she would with some witty Flout or other turn it off. Once I said, Child, *if you can't tell their Names, pray tell me what Clothes they have on?* And the Words were no sooner out of my Mouth, but she was laid for dead upon the Floor.

§ 23. One of the Spectators once asked her, *Whether she could not ride up stairs?* Unto which her Answer was, *That she believed she could, for her Horse could do very notable things.* Accordingly when her Horse came to her again, to our Admiration she Rode (that is, was tossed as one that rode) up the stairs: there then stood open the Study of one belonging to the Family, into which entering, she stood immediatly upon her Feet, and cryed out, *They are gone, they are gone! They say, that they cannot,* —— *God won't let 'em come here!* She also added a Reason for it which the Owner of the Study thought more kind than true. And she presently and perfectly came to her self, so that her whole Discourse and Carriage was altered unto the greatest measure of Sobriety, and she sat reading of the Bible and good Books, for a good part of the Afternoon. Her Affairs calling her anon to go down again, the Demons were in a quarter of a Minute, as bad upon her as before, and her Horse was waiting for her. I understanding of it, immediatly would have her up to the Study of the young man, where she had been at ease before: meerly to try whether there had not been a Fallacy in what had newly happened: but she was now so twisted and writhen that it gave me much trouble to get her into my Arms, and much more to drag her up the stairs. She was pulled out of my hands, and when I recovered my Hold, she was thrust so hard upon me, that I had almost fallen backwards, and her own Breast was sore afterwards, by their Compressions to detain her; she seem'd heavier indeed than three of her self. With incredible Forcing (though she kept Screaming *They say I must not go in*) at length we pull'd her in; where she was no sooner come, but she could stand on her Feet, and with an altered

Tone, could thank me, ſaying, now I am well. At firſt ſhee'd be ſomewhat faint, and ſay, ſhe felt ſomething go out of her; but in a Minute or two, ſhe could attend any Devotion, or Buſineſs, as well as ever in her life; and both ſpoke and did, as became a perſon of good Diſcretion.

I was loath to make a Charm of the Room, yet ſome ſtrangers that came to viſite us the Week after, deſiring to ſee the Experiment made, I permitted more than two or three Repetitions of it, and it ſtill ſucceeded as I have declared. Once when I was aſſiſting them in carrying of her up, ſhe was torn out of all our hands; and to my ſelf ſhe cry'd out, Mr. *M.*—— *One of them is going to puſh you down the ſtairs, have a care.* I remember not that I felt any Thruſt or Blow; but I think I was unaccountably made to ſtep down backward two or three ſtairs, & within a few hours ſhe told me by whom it was.

§ 24 One of thoſe that had been concerned for her Welfare, had newly Implored the great GOD, that the young Woman might be able to declare whom ſhe apprehended her ſelf troubled by. Preſently upon this her Horſe returned, only it peſtered her with ſuch ugly Paces, that ſhe fell out with her Company, and threatned now to tell all, for their ſo abuſing her. I was going abroad, and ſhe ſaid unto them that were about her, Mr. *M.*—— *is gone abroad, my horſe won't come back till he come home; and then I believe* (ſaid ſhe ſoftly) *I ſhall tell him all.* I ſtayed abroad an hour or two, and then returning; when I was juſt come to my Gate, before I had given the leaſt ſign or noiſe of my being there, ſhe ſaid, my Horſe is come! and Intimated that I was at the Door. When I came in, I found her mounted after her faſhion, upon her *Aerial Steed*, which carried her Fancy to the Journeys end. There (or rather then) ſhe maintained a conſiderable Diſcourſe with her Company, liſtening very attentively when ſhe had propounded any Queſtion, and receiving the Anſwers, with impreſſions made upon her mind. She ſaid, *Well what do you ſay? How many* *tis more am I to have? —— pray, can ye tell how long it all be before you are hang'd for what you have done? —— ou are filthy Witches to my knowledge, shall see some of you go after your sister, ou would have killed me, but you can't, don't fear you. —— You would have rown Mr.* Mather *down stairs, but u could not. —— Well! How shall I e * to morrow? Pray, What do you hink of to morrow? —— Fare ye well.*

Note, on to morrow the Ministers of the Town were to keep a day of Prayer at her Fathers house. *

—— *You have brought me such an ugly Horse, I am angry t you; I could find in my heart to tell all.* So she began er homeward paces; but when she had gone a little ay, (that is a little while) she said, *O I have forgot e Question, I must go back again;* and back she rides. he had that day been diverse times warning us, that hey had been contriving to do some harm to my Wife y a Fall or Blow, or the like; and when she came out f her mysterious Journeys, she would still be careful oncerning her. Accordingly she now calls to her Company again, Hark you, one thing more before we art! What hurt is it you will do to Mrs Mather? Will ou do her any hurt? Here she listened some time, and hen clapping her hands, cry'd out, O! I am glad on't, hey can do Mis. *Mather* no hurt: they try, but they say hey can't. So she returns, and at once dismissing her lorse and opening her Eyes, she call'd me to her; *Now ir (said she) I'le tell you all. I have learn'd who they re that are the cause of my trouble, ther's three of them, and she nam'd who) if they were out of the way, I should e well. They say, they can tell how long I shall be troubled, ut they won't. Only they seem to think their power will e broke this Week. They seem also to say, that I shall be ery ill to morrow; but they are themselves terribly afraid f to morrow, they fear that to morrow we shall be elivered. They say too, that they can't hurt Mrs.* Mather, *which I am glad of. But they said, they would kill me to ight, if I went to bed before ten a clock, if I t word*. And other things did ſhe ſay, not now to be recited:

§ 25. The day following, which was I think about the twenty ſeventh of *November*, Mr. *Morton* of *Charleſtown*, and Mr. *Allen*, Mr. *Moody*, Mr *Willard*, and my ſelf of *Boſton*, with ſome devout Neighbours, kept another Day of Prayer at *John Goodwin's* houſe, and we had all the Children preſent with us there: the Children were miſerably tortured while we laboured in our Prayers; but our good God was nigh unto us, in what we call'd upon him for. From this day the power of the Enemy was broken; and the children though Aſſaults after this were made upon them, yet were not ſo cruelly handled as before. The Liberty of the Children encreaſed daily more and more, and their Vexation abated by degrees; till within a little while they arrived to perfect eaſe, which for ſome Weeks or Months they cheerfully enjoyed. Thus *Good it is for us to draw near to God.*

§ 26. Within a day or two after the Faſt, the young Woman had two remarkable Attempts made upon her, by her inviſible Adverſaries: Once they were dragging her into the Oven that was then heating, while there was none in the Room to help her: ſhe clapt her hands on the Mantle-tree to ſave her ſelf, but they were beaten off; and ſhe had been burned, if at her Out-cries one had not come in from abroad for her relief. Another time they put an unſeen Rope with a cruel Nooſe about her Neck, whereby ſhe was choaked until ſhe was black in the Face; and though it was taken off before it had kill'd her, yet there was the red Marks of it, and a Finger and a Thumb near it, remaining to be ſeen for a while afterwards.

§ 27. This was the laſt Moleſtation that they gave her for a while, and ſhe dwelt at my houſe the reſt of the Winter, having by an obliging and vertuous Converſation, made her ſelf enough welcome to the Family; but within about a Fortnight, ſhe was viſited with two days of as extraordinary Obſeſſions, as any we had been the Spectators of. I thought it convenient for me, to entertain my Congregation with a Sermon, upon the memorable Providences which these Children had been concerned in. When I had begun to study my Sermon, her Tormentors again seiz'd upon her; and all *Fryday* and *Saturday* did they manage her, with a special Design as was plain, to disturb me in what I was about. In the worst of her Extravagancies, formerly she was more dutiful to my self than I had reason to expect, but now her whole carriage to me, was with a Sauciness that I had not been us'd to be treated with. She would knock at my Study door, affirming that some below would be glad to see me, when there was none that ask't for me. She would call to me with multiplying Impertinencies, and throw small things at me, wherewith she could not give me any hurt. Shee'd hector me at a strange rate, for the work I was at, and threaten me with I know not what mischief for it. She got a History that I had written of this Witchcraft, and though she had before this, read it over and over, yet now she could not read (I believe) one entire Sentence of it; but she made of it the most ridiculous *Travestry* in the World, with such a Patness and excess of Fancy, to supply the sense that she put upon it, as I was amazed at. And she particularly told me, that I should quickly come to disgrace by that History.

§ 28. But there were many other Wonders beheld by us before these two days were out. Few tortures attended her, but such as were provoked; her Frolicks being the things that had most possession of her. I was in Latine, telling some young Gentlemen of the Colledge, That if I should bid her look to God, her eyes would be put out, upon which her eyes were presently served so. I was in some surprize when I saw that her Troublers understood Latine, and it made me willing to try a little more of their Capacity. We continually found, that if an *English Bible* were in any part of the Room seriously look'd into, though she saw and heard nothing

nothing of it, she would immediatly be in very dism Agonies. We now made a Tryal more than once or twice of the Greek New Testament, and the Hebre Old Testament; and we still found, That if one shoul go to read in it never so secretly, and silently, it woul procure her that Anguish, which there was no endurin of. But I thought at length, I fell upon one inferio Language, which the Dæmons did not seem so well t understand.

§. 29. Devotion was now as formerly, the terriblest of all the Provocations that could be given her. I coul by no means, bring her to owne that she desirea th Mercies of God, and the Prayers of good men. I woul have obtained a Sign of such a desire, by her lifting up of her hand, but she stirred it not: I then lifted up her hand my self, and though the standers by, thought a more insignificant thing could not be propounded, I said, Child, if you desire those things, let your hand fall when I take mine away: I took my hand away, and hers continued strangely and stifly stretched out, so that for some time she could not take it down. During these two days, we had Prayers oftner in our Family than at other times; and this was her usual Behaviour at them. The man that prayed, usually began with reading the Word of God; which once as he was going to do, she call'd to him, read of *Mary Magdalen, out of whom the Lord cast seven devils.* During the time of reading, she would be laid as one fast asleep; but when Prayer was begun, the Devils would still throw her on the Floor, at the feet of him that prayed: There would she ly, and Whistle and sing and roar, to drown the voice of the Prayer; but that being a little too audible for them, they would shut close her Mouth and her Ears, and yet make such odd noises in her Throat, as that she her self could not hear our Cries to God for her. Shee'd also fetch very terrible Blows with her Fist, and Kicks with her Foot at the man that prayed; but still (for he had bid that none should hinder her) her Fist and Foot would

would always recoil, when they came within a few hairs breadths of him, just as if Rebounding against a Wall; so that she touched him not, but then would beg hard of other people to strike him, and particularly she entreated them to take the Tongs and smite him; Which not being done, she cryed out of him, he has wounded me in the Head. But before Prayer was out, she would be laid for Dead, wholly senseless, and (unless to a severe Trial) breathless, with her Belly swelled like a Drum, and sometimes with croaking Noises in it; thus would she ly, most exactly with the stiffness and posture of one that had been two Days laid out for Dead. Once lying thus, as he that was praying, was alluding to the words of the *Canaanitess*, and saying, *Lord, have mercy on a Daughter vexed with a Devil*; there came a big, but low voice from her, saying, *There's two or three of them*, (*or us!*) and the standers by, were under that Apprehension, as that they cannot relate whether her mouth mov'd in speaking of it. When Prayer was ended, she would Revive in a Minute or two, and continue as Frolicksome as before: she thus continued until *Saturday* towards the Evening; when, after this man had been at Prayer, I charged all my Family to admit of no Diversion by her Frolicks, from such exercises as it was proper to begin the Sabbath with. They took the Counsel, and though she essayed, with as witty, and as nimble, and as various an Application to each of them successively, as ever I saw, to make them laugh, yet they kept close to their good Books, which then called for their Attention: when she saw that, immediatly she fell asleep, and in two or three hours she waked perfectly her self; weeping bitterly to remember (for as one come out of a Dream she could remember) what had befallen her.

§ 30. After this, we had no more such entertainments. The Demons it may be, would once or twice in a Week trouble her for a few Minuts, with perhaps a twisting and a twinkling of her eyes; or a certain Cough, which did seem to be more than ordinary. Moreover, both

She at my house, and her Sister at home, at the tin which they call *Christmass*, were by the Demons mac very drunk, though they had no strong Drink (as w are fully sure) to make them so. When she began t feel her self thus drunk, she complain'd, O they sa they will have me to keep *Christmass* with them! the will disgrace me when they can do nothing else! An immediatly the ridiculous Behaviours of one drunl were with a wonderful exactness represented in he Speaking, and Reeling, and Spewing, and anon Sleep ing, till she was well again. But the Vexations of th Children otherwise abated continually.

They first came to be always quiet, unless upon Pro vocations. Then they got liberty to work, but not to read: then further on, to read, but not aloud. At last they were wholly delivered, and for many Weeks re mained so.

§ 31. I was not unsensible, that it might be an easie thing to be too bold, and go too far, in making of Experiments: nor was I so unphilosophical, as not to discern many opportunities in Giving and Solving many Problems, which the *Pneumatick Discipline* is concerned in. I confess I have learn'd much more than I sought; and I have been informed of some things relating to the invisible World, which as I did not think it lawful to ask, so I do not think it proper to tell; yet I will give a Touch upon one Problem commonly discoursed of; that is,

Whether the Devils know our Thoughts, or no?

I will not give the Reader my Opinion of it, but only my Experiment. That they do not, was conjectured from this: We could cheat them when we spoke one thing, and mean't another. This was found when the Children were to be undressed. The Devils would still in ways, beyond the Force of any Imposture, wonderfully twist the part that was to be undressed, so that there was no coming at it. But, if we said, untye this Neck cloth, and the Parties bidden

at

at the same time, understood our intent to be, unty his Shoe! The Neck-cloth and not the Shoe, has been made strangely inaccessible. But on the other side, That they do, may be Conjectured from this: I called the young Woman at my House by her Name, intending to mention unto her some Religious Expedient, whereby she might as I thought, much relieve her self; presently her Neck was broke, and I continued watching my Opportunity, to say what I designed. I could not get her to come out of her Fit, until I had laid aside my purpose of speaking what I thought, and then she reviv'd immediatly. Moreover a young Gentleman visiting of me at my Study, to ask my Advice about curing the Atheism and Blasphemy, which he complained his Thoughts were more than ordinarily then infested with; after some Discourse, I carried him down to see this Girl, who was then molested with her unseen Fiends; but when he came, she treated him very coursly and rudely, asking him what he came to the house for? and seemed very angry at his being there, urging him to be gone, with a very impetuous Importunity. Perhaps all Devils are not alike sagacious.

§ 32. The last Fit that the young Woman had, was very peculiar. The Demons having once again seiz'd her, they made her pretend to be Dying; and Dying, truly we fear'd at last she was: She lay, she tossed, she pull'd just like one Dying, and urged hard for some one to dye with her, seeming loth to dye alone. She argued concerning Death, in strains that quite amazed us; and concluded, that though she was loth to Die, yet if God said she must, she must; adding something about the state of the Countrey, which we wondered at. Anon, the Fit went over, and as I guessed it would be, it was the last fit she had at our house. But all my Library never afforded me any Commentary on those Paragraphs of the Gospels, which speak of Demoniacks, equal to that which the Passions of this Child have given me.

§ 33.

§ 33. This is the Story of *Goodwins* Children, a St[...] all made up of Wonders! I have related nothing [...] what I judge to be true. I was my ſelf an Eye-witn[...] to a large part of what I tell; and I hope my Neighbo[...] have long thought, that I have otherwiſe learned Chr[...] than to lie unto the World. Yea, there is I belie[...] ſcarce any one particular in this Narrative, which mo[...] than one credible Witneſs will not be ready to ma[...] Oath unto; the things of moſt concernment in it, we[...] before many Critical Obſervers; and the whole happe[...] ed in the *Metropolis* of the *Engliſh America*, unto a relig[...] ous and induſtrious Family, which was viſited by all ſo[...] of Perſons, that had a mind to ſatisfie themſelves. I [...] now likewiſe Publiſh the Hiſtory, while the thing is y[...] freſh and new; and I challenge all men to detect ſo mu[...] as one deſigned Falſhood; yea, or ſo much as one im[...] portant Miſtake, from the Egg to the Apple of it. I ha[...] Writ as plainly as becomes an Hiſtorian, as truly as b[...] comes a Chriſtian, though perhaps not ſo profitably [...] became a Divine. But I am reſolv'd after this, never [...] uſe but juſt one Grain of Patience with any man that ſh[...] go to impoſe upon me, a Denial of Devils, or of Witc[...] es. I ſhal count that man Ignorant who ſhal ſuſpect b[...] I ſhal count him down right Impudent, if he Aſſert th[...] Non-Exiſtence of things which we have had ſuch palpab[...] Convictions of. I am ſure he cannot be a Civil, (an[...] ſome will queſtion, whether he can be an honeſt man[...] that ſhal go to deride the Being of things which a whol[...] Countrey has now beheld, an Houſe of pious People ſu[...] fering not a few Vexations by. But if the Sadducee [...] the Atheiſt, have no right Impreſſions by theſe Memora[...] ble Providences made upon his Mind; yet I hope, tho[...] that know what it is to be ſober, will not repent an[...] pains that they may have taken, in peruſing what Re[...] cords of theſe Witchcrafts and Poſſeſſions, I thus leav[...] unto Poſterity.

POSTSCRIPT

POSTSCRIPT.

YOu have seen the Trouble and the Relief of *John Goodwins* Children; after which the Demons were let loose to make a fresh Attempt upon them, though not in a manner altogether so terrib'e and afflictive, as what they had before sustained. All the three Children were visited with some Return of their Calamities; but the Boy was the Child which endured most in this new Assault: He had been for some while kindly entertained with Mr. *Bailly* at *Watertown*, where he had enjoyed a long time of ease; the Devils having given him but a little Disturbance, except what was for a short while after his first coming there. He no sooner came Home, but he began to be ill again, with diverse peculiar Circumstances attending of him. There was this particularly remarkable, that the Boy dream'd he had a Bone within his Skin growing cross his Ribs; and when he awaked, he felt and found a thing there, which was esteemed a Bone by them that handled it; only every one wondered how it should be lodged there. An expert Chirurgion, Dr. *John Clark*, being Advised with about it, very dexterously took it out; and it prov'd not the imagined Bone, but a considerable Pin; a Brass Pin, which could not possibly have come to ly there as it did, without the prestigious Conveyance of a mysterious Witchcraft. Another time on a Lords day, his Father would have taken him to Meeting with him; and when his Father spoke of going to some of the Assemblies in the Town, (particularly both the North and the South) the Boy would be cast into such Tortures and Postures, that he would sooner Die than go out of Doors; but if his Father spoke of going to others of the Assemblies in the Town, particularly the *Quakers*, the Boy in a moment, would be as well as could be. The tryal of this was more than five times Repeated, and were it fully related, would be more than ten times Admired.

Our

Our Prayers for the Children were justly renew and I hope not altogether unanswered. Upon one Pr er over two of them, they had about a Fortnights ea and their Ails again returning, Prayer was again awak ed; with some Circumstances not proper to be expo unto the World. God gave a present Abatement he upon to the Maladies of the Children, and caused th Invaders to retire; so that by degrees they were fu and quickly delivered. Two days of Prayer obtain the Deliverance of two. The third namely the Bo remaining under some Annoyance by the evil spirits, third day was employ'd for him, and he soon found t blessed Effects of it in his Deliverance also. There we several very memorable things attending this Delive ance of the Children, and the Vows, and the Pleas, us in the Prayers which were thereby Answered, but th were all private, yea, in a sort Secret; *Non est Relig ubi omnia patent*. And I understand, (for I have som Acquaintance with him) that the Friend of the Ch dren, whom God gave to be thus concerned and succe ful for them, desires me not to let Reports of those thin go out of the Walls of a Study, but to leave them rath for the notice of the other World. I think it will not b improper to tell the World, that one thing in the Chi drens Deliverance, was the strange Death of an horrib old Woman, who was presum'd to have a great hand i their Affliction: before her Death and at it, the Alm house where she lived, was terrified with fearful Nois and she seem'd to have her Death hastned by dism Blows, received from the invisible World. But havi mentioned this, all that I have now to publish, is, th Prayer and Faith, was the thing that drove the Dev from the Children; and I am to bear this Testimony u to the World, *That the Lord is nigh to all them that ca upon him in truth, and, That blessed are all they that wa for him.*

Finished, *June 7th*, 1689.

MANTISSA

MANTISSA.

TO the foregoing Narrative, we have added an account given us by the Godly Father of these Haunted Children; who upon his Reading over so much our History, as was written of their Exercise before their [...]*ll deliverance, was willing to express his Attestation to* [...]*e Truth of it; with this further Declaration of the Sense,* [...]*hich he had of the unusual Miseries, that then lay upon his* [...]*amily. 'Tis in his own Style; but I suppose a Pen hath not* [...]*mmonly been managed with more cleanly Discourse by an* [...]*and used only to the Trowel; and his Condition hath been* [...]*ch, that he may have fairly have Leave to speak.*

IN the year 1688, about Midsummer, it pleased the Lord to visit one of my Children with a sore Visitation; and she was not only Tormented in her Body, but was in great distress of Mind, Crying out, *That she was in the dark concerning her Souls estate, and* [...]*hat she had mispent her precious time*; She and we thin[...]king her time was near at an end: Hearing those Shricks [...]nd Groans which did not only pierce the Ears, but [...]Hearts of her poor Parents; now was a time for me to Consider with my self, and to look into my own heart [...]nd life, and see how matters did there stand between God and my own soul, and see *Wherefore the Lord was thus* [...]*ontending with me.* And upon Enquiry I found cause to judge my self, and to justifie the Lord. This affli[...]ction continuing some time, the Lord saw good then to double the affliction in smiting down another Child, and that which was most heart-breaking of all, and did double this double affliction was, it was apparent and judged by all that saw them, that the Devil and his Instruments, had a hand in it.

The consideration of this was most dreadful: I thought

of what *David* said, 2 *Sam.* 24. 14. if he feared so to fall into the hands of Men, oh! then to think of the Horror of our condition, to be in the hands of Devils and Witches! This our doleful condition moved us to call to our Friends to have pity on us, for *Gods Hand had touched us*. I was ready to say, that no ones affliction was like mine; That my little House that should be a little *Bethel* for God to dwell in, should be made a Den for Devils; that those little Bodies, that should be Temples for the Holy Ghost to dwell in, should be thus harrassed & abused by the Devil & his cursed Brood But now this twice doubled affliction is doubled again. Two more of my Children are smitten down, oh! the Cries, the Shricks, the Tortures of these poor Children! Doctors cannot help, Parents weep and lament over them, but cannot ease them. Now I considering my affliction to be more than ordinary, it did certainly call for more than ordinary Prayer. I acquainted Mr. *Allen*, Mr. *Moodey*, Mr. *Willard*, and Mr. *C. Mather*, the four Ministers of the Town with it, and Mr. *Morton* of *Charlstown*; earnestly desiring them, that they, with some other praying people of God, would meet at my house, and there be earnest with God, on the behalf of us and our Children; which they (I thank them for it) readily attended with great fervency of Spirit; but as for my part, my heart was ready to sink to hear and see those doleful Sights. Now I thought that I had greatly neglected my duty to my Children, in not admonishing and instructing of them; and that God was hereby calling my sins to mind, to slay my Children, Then I pondered of that place in Numb. 23. 23. *Surely there is no Inchantment against Jacob, neither is there any Divination against Israel.* And now I thought I had broke Covenant with God, not only in one respect but in many, but it pleased the Lord to bring that to mind in *Heb.* 8. 12. *For I will be merciful to their unrighteousness, and their Sins and Iniquities will I remember no more.* The Consideration how the Lord

did

did deal with *Job*, and his Patience and the End the Lord made with him was some support to me. I thought also, on what *David* said, that *he had sinned, but what have these poor Lambs done?* But yet in the midst of my tumultuous Thoughts within me, it was Gods Comfort that did delight my soul. That in the 18 of *Luke*, and the beginning, Where Christ spake the Parable for that end, that men ought *always to pray and not faint.* This, with many other places bore up my spirit. I thought with *Jonah* that I *would yet again look towards God's holy Temple; the Lord Jesus Christ.* And I did greatly desire to find the Son of God with me in this Furnace of Affliction, knowing hereby that no harm shall befall me. But now this solemn day of Prayer and Fasting being at an End, there was an eminent Answer of it: for one of my Children was delivered, and one of the wicked Instruments of the Devil discovered, and her own mouth condemned her, and so accordingly Executed. Here was Food for Faith, and great encouragement still to *hope and quietly wait for the Salvation of the Lord*; the Ministers still counselling and encouraging me to labour to be found in Gods way, committing my case to him, and not to use any way not allowed in Gods Word. It was a thing not a little comfortable to us, to see that the people of God was so much concerned about our lamentable condition, remembring us at all times in their prayers, which I did look at as a token for good; but you must think it was a time of sore Temptation with us, for many did say, (yea, and some good people too) were it their case, that they would try some Tricks, that should give ease to their children: But I thought for us to forsake the counsel of good old men, and to take the counsel of the young ones, it might ensnare our souls, though for the present it might offer some relief to our Bodies; which was a thing I greatly feared; and my Children were not at any time [illegible] doing any such thing. It was a time of so[illegible] was mixed with abundance of mercy, for my heart was many a time made glad in the house of Prayer. The Neighbourhood pitied us, and were very helpful to us: Moreover, though my Children were thus in every Limb and Joynt tormented by those Children of the Devil, they also using their tongues at their pleasure sometimes one way, sometimes another; yet the Lord did herein prevent them, that they could not make them speak wicked words, though they did many times hinder them from speaking good ones; had they in these Fits blaspheme the Name of the Holy God this you may think would have been an heart-breaking thing to us the poor Parents; but God in his mercy prevented them, a thing worth taking notice of: Likewise they slept well all night: And the Ministers did often visit us, and pray with us, and for us; and their love and pity was so great, their Prayers so earnest and constant, that I could not but admire at it. Mr. *Mather* particularly; now his bowels so yearned towards us in this sad condition, that he not only prays with us, and for us, but he taketh one of my Children home to his own house; which indeed was but a troublesome guest, for such an one that had so much work lying upon his hands and heart: He took much pains in this great Service, to pull this Child, and her Brother and Sisters out of the hand of the Devil. Let us now admire and adore that Fountain the Lord Jesus Christ, from whence those streams come. The Lord himself will requite his labour of love. Our case is yet very sad, and doth call for more Prayer; and the good Ministers of this Town, and *Charlstown* readily came, with some other good praying people to my house, to keep another Day of solemn Fasting and Prayer; which our Lord saith this *kind goeth out by*. My Children being all at home the two biggest lying on the bed, one of them would fain have Kicked the good men while they were wrestling with Go[d for] them, had not I held him with ll my power and might; and sometimes he would stop his own ears. This you must needs think was a cutting thing to the poor Parents. Now our hearts were ready to sink, had not God put under his everlasting arms of Mercy and helped us still to hope in his mercy, and to be quiet, knowing that He is God, and that it was not for the potsheards of the earth to strive with their Maker. Well might *David* say, that had not the *Law of his God been his delight, he had perished in his affliction.* Now the Promises of God are sweet; God having promised, to *hear the prayer of the destitute,* and *not to despise their prayer*; and *He will not fail in the Expectation of those that wait on Him*; but He *heareth the cry of the poor and needy.* These *Jacobs* came and wrestled with God for a blessing on this poor Family, which indeed I hope they obtained, and may be now worthy of the Name *Israel*, who prevailed with God, and *would not let Him go till He had blessed us.* For soon after this, there were two more of my Children delivered out of this horrible pit. Here was now a double mercy, and how sweet was it, knowing it came in Answer of Prayer! Now we see and know, it is not a vain thing to call on the name of the Lord. For he is a present help in the time of trouble; and we may boldly say the Lord has been our helper. I had sunk, but Jesus put forth his hand and bore me up. My Faith was ready to fail, but this was a support to me that Christ said to *Peter, I have prayed for thee that thy faith fail not.* And many other *Promises* were as Cordials to my drooping Soul. And the Consideration of all those that ever came to Christ Jesus for Healing, that he healed their bodies, pardoned their Sins, and healed their Souls too; which I hope in God may be the fruit of this present Affliction. If God be pleased to make the Fruit of this Affliction to be to take away our sin, and cleanse us from iniquity, and to put us on with greater diligence to *make our Calling and Election sure,* then, happy Affliction! The Lord said that I had need of this to awake me. I have found a prosperous Condition a dangerous Conditio I have taken notice and considered more of God Goodness in these few weeks of Affliction, than in m ny years of Prosperity. I may speak it with shame, wicked and deceitful, and ungrateful is my hear that the more God hath been doing for me, the less have been doing for Him. My Returns have not bee according to my Receivings. The Lord help me now praise Him in heart, lip, and life. The Lord help us see by this Visitation, what need we have to get she ter under the wing of Christ, to haste to the Rock, whe we may be safe. We see how ready the Devils a to catch us, and torment our Bodies, and he is as di gent to ensnare our Souls, and that many ways; b let us put on all our spiritual Armour, and follow Chri the Captain of our Salvation; and though we meet wit the Cross, let us bear it patiently and cheerfully, fo if Jesus Christ be at the one end, we need not fear th Heft of it: if we have Christ we have enough; H can make His Rod as well as His Staff to be a com fort to us; and we shall not want if we be the Sheep o Christ. If we want Afflictions we shall have them, an sanctified Afflictions are choice mercies.

Now I earnestly desire the Prayer of all good People That the Lord would be pleased to perfect that Work H hath begun, and make it to appear that Prayer is stron ger than Witchcraft.

John Goodwin.

Decemb. 12. 1688.

This is our First Example; and it is This which has occa sioned the Publication of the Rest.

EXAMPLE

EXAMPLE. II.

AMong those Judgments of God, which are a great Deep, I suppose few are are more unfathomable than this, That Pious and Holy Men suffer sometimes by the Force of horrid Witchcrafts, and Hellish Witches are permitted to break thorow the Hedge which our Heavenly Father has made about them that seek Him. I suppose the Instances of this direful thing are Seldom; but that they are not Never we can produce very dismal Testimony. One, and that no less Recent than Awful, I shall now offer: and the Reader of it will thereby learn, I hope, to *work out his own Salvation with Fear and Trembling*.

§. 1. Mr. *Philip Smith*, aged about Fifty years, a Son of eminently vertuous Parents, a Deacon of the Church at *Hadley*, a Member of our General Court, an Associat in their County Court, a Select man for the affairs of the Town, a Lieutenant in the Troop, and, which crowns all, a man for Devotion and Gravity, and all that was Honest, exceeding Exemplary: Such a man in the Winter of the Year 1684, was murdered with an hideous Witchcraft, which filled all those parts with a just astonishment. This was the manner of the Murder.

§. 2. He was concerned about Relieving the Indigencies of a wretched Woman in the Town; who being dissatisfied at some of his just cares about her, expressed her self unto him in such a manner, that he declared himself apprehensive of receiving mischief at her hands; he said, he doubted she would attempt his Hurt.

§. 3. About the beginning of *January* he began to be very Valetudinarious, labouring under those that termed Ischiadick Pains. As his Illness increased on him, so his Goodness increased in him; the standers by could in him see one ripening apace for another World, and one filled not only with Grace to an high degree, but also with exceeding Joy. Such Weanedne from, and Weariness of the World, he shew'd, th. he knew not (he said) whether he might pray for h continuance here. Such Assurance had he of th Divine Love unto him, that in Raptures he woul cry out, *Lord, stay thine hand, it is enough, it is mo than thy frail servant can bear!* But in the midst of the things, he uttered still an hard suspicion, That the i Woman who had treatned him, had made impressio on him.

§. 4. While he remained yet of a sound mind, l very sedately, but very solemnly, charged his Broth to look well after him. Tho' he said he now understoo himself, yet he knew not how he might be; *but be su* (said he) *to have a care of me for you shall see strange thing There shall be a wonder in* Hadley! *I shall not be dead wh it is thought I am!* This Charge he pressed over and o ver; and afterwards became Delirious.

§. 5. Being become Delirious, he had a Speech in cessant and Voluble beyond all imagination, and th in diverse Tones and sundry Voices, and (as wa thought) in various Languages.

§. 6. He cryed out not only of sore Pains, but als of sharp Pins, pricking of him: sometimes in his To sometimes in his Arm, as if there had been hundred of them. But the people upon search never found an more than One.

§. 7. In his Distresses he exclaimed very much upo the Woman afore-mentioned, naming her, and som others, and saying, *Do you not see them; There, Ther there they stand.*

§. 8. There was a strong smell of something lik Musk, which was diverse times in the Room where h was, and in the other Rooms, and without the Hous of which no cause could be rendred. The sick man a well as others, complained of it; and once particula ly, it so seiz'd an Apple Roasting at the Fire, th they were forced to throw it away.

§. 9. Som

§ 9. Some that were about him, being almost at their ... end, by beholding the greatness and the strangeness of his Calamities, did three or four times in one Night, go and give Disturbance to the Woman that we have spoken of: all the while they were doing of it, the good man was at ease, and slept as a weary man; and these were all the times they perceived him to take any sleep at all.

§ 10. A small Galley-Pot of *Alkermes* that was near full, and carefully look't after, yet unto the surprize of the people, was quite emptied, so that the sick man could not have the Benefit of it.

§ 11. Several persons that sat by him, heard a Scratching, that seem'd to be on the Ticking near his Feet, while his Feet lay wholly still; nay, were held in the hands of others, and his hands were far off another way.

§ 12. Sometimes Fire was seen on the Bed or the Covering, and when the Beholders began to Discourse of it, it would vanish away.

§ 13. Diverse people felt something often stir in the Bed, at some distance from his Body; to appearance, the thing that stirred, was as big as a Cat: some tryed to lay hold on it with their hands, but under the Covering nothing could be found. A discreet and sober Woman resting on the Beds feet, felt as it were a Hand, the Thumb and the Finger of it, taking her by the Side, and giving her a *Pinch*; but turning to see what it might be, nothing was to be seen.

§ 14. The Doctor standing by the sick man, and seeing him ly still, he did himself try to lean on the Beds head, but he found the Bed to shake so, that his Head was often knocked against the *Post*, though he strove to hold it still; and others upon Tryal found the same Also the sick man lying too near the side of the Bed, a very strong and stout man, try'd to lift him a little further into the Bed, but with all his might he could not; though trying by and by, he could lift a Bed-stead with a Bed, and a man lying on it, all, without any *Strain* to himself at all.

§ 15.

§ 15. Mr. *Smith* Dies: the Jury that viewed
Corps, found a Swelling on one Breast, which render
it like a Womans: his Privities were wounded or burn
on his Back besides Bruises, there were several *Pricks*
Holes, as if done with Awls or Pins.

§ 16. After the Opinion of all had pronounc'd hi
dead, his Countenance continued as Lively, as if he h
been Alive; his Eyes closed as in a slumber, and his
ther Jaw not falling down. Thus he remained from
nday Morning about Sun-rise, till *Sabbath-day* in t
Afternoon. When those that took him out of the B
found him still warm, though the Season was as cold,
had almost been known in an Age. On the night after t
Sabbath, his Countenance was yet as fresh as before;
on *Monday* morning, they found the Face extremely
mified and discoloured; 'twas black and blue, and fre
Blood seem'd to run down his Cheek in the Hairs.

§ 17. The night after he died, a very credible pers
watching of the Corps, perceived the Bed to move an
stir, more than once; but by no means could find
the cause of it.

§ 18 The second night, some that were preparing f
the Funeral, do say, That they heard diverse Noises
Room where the Corps lay, as though there had been
great Removing, and Clattering of Stools and Chairs.

Upon the whole, it appeared unquestionable, th
Witchcraft had brought a Period unto the life of so go
a man.

EXAMPLE III.

THe man of whom we have been writing, is not t
only good Christian whom vile Witchcraft has giv
Annoyance to. *We* shall add a second Instanc
wherein I shall Relate something that I do not Approv
and that is, the Urinary Experiment. I suppose the Uri
must be Bottled with Nails and *Pins*, and such Instr
men

ments in it, as carry a Shew of Torture with them, if it attain its End. For I have been told, that the bare Bottleing of Urine with Filings of Steel in it, which can be better (though scarce well) accounted for, has been found insignificant. Now, to use a Charm against a Charm, or to use a Devils *Shield* against a Devils Sword, who can with a good Conscience try? All Communion with Hell is dangerous, all Relief and Succour coming by means, whose whole Force is founded in the Laws of the Kingdom of Darkness, will be ready to leave a Sting on the Conscience of him that obtains it so.

§ 1. There was one Mr. *St*.---*n* of *North-hampton*, who upon Complaint of an abused Servant unto him, had in plain and close Terms, rebuked the Master of the Lad, for his too great Severity: he was a man of good Repute, and as good Courage; but within as little a while as the man whom he had reproved could return to inform his VVife, who was a person under Suspicion for VVitchcraft, he was taken with many Ails and pains, that increased on him to great Extremity.

§ 2. He languishes, decays, and dies: but before it came to that, strange Sights were in the house. A black Cat appeared in the night, with very affrighting Circumstances; and then a Pigeon; both of which they pursued in vain, though both of them were in the house.

§ 3. They went to the Traditional Experiment of Bottling Urine, but they could get no Urine from him: a strange Hole through the Urinary *Passage* shedding the Water before they could receive it into the Vessel.

§ 4. The Corps was viewed by the Jury; an Hole was found quite through his Yard, which hindered their saving of any Urine, and gave a terrible Torture to him: about the small of his Back, there was a multitude of small Spots, the Callous out side of which, being taken away, underneath were Holes, as though made by small Shot. Upon which all concluded with good Reason, the Occasion of his Death to be something preternatural.

EXAMPLE

EXAMPLE IV.

SO Horrid and Hellish is the Crime of Witchcraft, th were Gods Thoughts as our thoughts, and God Ways as our ways, it could be no other but unpardon able. But that the Grace of God may be admired, an that the worst of Sinners may be encouraged, Behold Witchcraft also has found a Pardon. Let no man de pair of his own Forgiveness, but let no man also dela about his own Repentance, how aggravated soever hi Transgressions are. From the Hell of Witchcraft ou merciful Jesus can fetch a guilty Creature to the Glory o Heaven. Our LORD hath sometimes Recovered those who have in the most horrid manner, given themselve away to the Destroyer of their souls.

§ 1. There was one *Mary Johnson*, tryed at *Hartfor* in this Countrey, upon an Indictment of Familiarit with the Devil; she was found Guilty of the sam chiefly upon her own Confession, and condemned.

§ 2. Many years are past since her Execution, an the Records of the Court are but short; yet there a several Memorables that are found credibly Related an Attested concerning her.

§ 3. She said, that a Devil was wont to do her man Services. Her Master once blam'd her for not carryi out the Ashes, and a Devil did clear the Hearth for h afterwards. Her Master sending her into the Field, drive out the Hogs that us'd to break into it, a Dev would scowre them out, and make her laugh to see ho he feaz'd them about.

§ 4. Her first Familiarity with the Devils came by di content, and wishing the Devils to take that and t'oth thing, and the Devil to do this and that; whereupon Devil appeared unto her, tendring her the best Servi he cou'd do for her.

§ 5. She confessed that she was guilty of the Murd of a Child, and that she had been guilty of Uncleann with Men and Devils.

§

§. 6. In the time of her Imprisonment, the famous Mr. *Samuel Stone* was at great pains to promote her Conversion unto God, and represent unto her both her Misery and Remedy; the Success of which, was very desireable, and considerable.

§. 7. She was by most Observers judged very Penitent, both before and at her Execution; and she went out of the World with many Hopes of Mercy through the Merit of Jesus Christ, Being asked, *What she built her hopes upon*; She answered, on those Words, *Come to me all ye that labour and are heavy laden, and I will give you Rest*; and those, *There is a Fountain open for Sin and for Uncleanness.* And she died in a Frame extreamly to the satisfaction of them that were Spectators of it.

Our GOD is a great Forgiver.

EXAMPLE V.

THe near Affinity between Witchcraft and Possession, invites me to add unto the foregoing Histories, one that the Reader, I believe, will count worthy to be Related. It is but a Fragment of what should have been a fuller Story; but I cannot without some Trouble or Delay inconsistent with my present Designs put my self in a way to perfect it: and I was of the Opinion, that, *Let nothing be lost*, was a Rule which I might very properly extend unto it. The thing happened many (perhaps thirty) Years ago, and was then much discoursed of. I don't Remember, that I have heard what became of the Boy concerned in the Narrative, but what I now publish, I find among the Papers of my Grand-Father, of whom the World has had such a Character, that they cannot but judge, no Romance or Folly, nothing but what should be serious and weighty could be worthy of His Hand; and it is in his own Hand that I have the Manuscript, from whence I have caused it to be Transcribed. It runs in such Terms as these.

A Confeſſion of a Boy at Tocutt; *in the time of the Intermiſſion of his Fits: and other Paſſages, which many were Eye-witneſſes of.*

THe Boy was for his natural Parts, more than ord nary at ſeven years old. He, with many othe went to ſee a Conjurer play Tricks in *Holland*. The it was ſtrongly ſuggeſted to him, He ſhould be as goo an Artiſt as he. From thence to eleven years old, he ſed the Trade of inventing Lyes, and Stealing Mone Running away from his Father, ſpending of it at Dic and with the vileſt Company; and this Trade he uſe in that ſpace (he confeſſed) above Fourty times at lea and many ſtrange Inſtances he gives of it. His Fath following him with conſtant Inſtruction, and Correctio he was deſperatly hardned under all, and his hea ſet in a way of Malice againſt the Word of God, an all his Father did to reſtrain him. When he w about ten or eleven years old, he ran away from *Rotte dam*, to *Delph*; and the Devil appeared to him the in the Shape of a Boy, counſelling him not to hearke to the Word of God, nor unto any of his Father's I ſtructions, and propounding to him, to Enter into Covenant with him. Being ſomewhat fearful at fir deſired that he would not appear to him in a Shape, b by a Voice, and though his heart did inwardly conſen to what the Devil ſaid, yet he was withheld that could not then Enter into a Covenant with him. H Father not knowing this, but of his other Wickedne being a Godly Miniſter, procured many Chriſtians join with him in a day of Humiliation; confeſſed a bewailed his Sins, prayed for him, and ſent him to *Ne E*. and ſo committed him to God. From that time this being now about Sixteen Years old, the Dev hath conſtantly come to him by a Voice; and he he a conſtant Diſcourſe with him; and all about Entri into a Covenant with him: and ſtill perſwaded to ha it Written and Sealed, making many Promises to allure him, and telling him many Stories of Doctor *Faustus*, and other Witches how bravely they have lived, and how he should live deliciously, and have Ease, Comfort, and Money; and sometimes threatning to tear him in pieces if he would not. But ordinarily his discourses was as loving and friendly as could be. He hath been strangely kept, by an hand of God, from making a Covenant to this day. For he still propounded many Difficulties to the Devil, which he could not satisfie his Reason in: and though, he saith, he was never well but when he was Discoursing with the Devil, and his heart was strangely enclined to Write and Seal an Agreement, yet such dreadful horrour did seize upon him, at the very time, from the Word of God, and such fears of his Eternal Perishing, that he could not do it then. He put off the Devil still, that he was not in a fit frame, but desired him to come again that he might have more Discourse, and he would consider of it. The Devil appeared to him a second time at *New-haven*, in the Shape of a Boy, and a third time at *Tocutt* in the Shape of a Fox; at which time, at first, they had loving discourse, as formerly; but at last, the Devil was urgent upon him, and told him, he had baffled with him so long, now he must enter into an agreement, or he would tear him in pieces: he saying, *How should I do it? would ye have me write upon my hands? No,* (saith the Devil) *look here*, and with that, set Paper, and Pen, and Ink like Blood before him. The former horrours, from the Word of God, and special Passages, which he named, set in upon him so that he could not do it. Only before they parted, the Devil being so urgent upon him, telling him he had baffled with him, he set a year and half time for Consideration. The last quarter of a year is yet to come. The Devil told him, if he let him alone so long, he would baffle with him still: he answered, if he did not yield then, he would give him leave to torment him whilst he lived. Still the Devil would not away, nor could he get from him. Then out of Fear he cryed out, *Lord, Jesus, rebuke the Devil*! at which, the Fox, Pen, Ink and Paper vanished. Yet he continued in his course of unheard of Wickedness, and still his Will was bent to Write and Seal the Agreement, having his Discourse yet with Satan by Voice. His Brother with whom he lives at *Tocutt*, having Convulsion Fits, he laughed and mocked at him, and acted the Convulsion Fits. A while after God sent Convulsion Fits on him-self; in which time, his former Terrours, the Wrath God, Death, Hell, Judgment, and Eternity were pre-sented to him. He would fain then have confessed his sins, but when he was about to do it, the Devil still held his mouth, that he could not. He entreated God, to release him, promising to confess and forsake his Sins and the Lord did so; but he being well, grew as bad, or worse than ever. About six weeks since, his Covulsion Fits came again three times most dreadfully,, with some Intermissions. and his former Horrours and Fears He would have confessed his Sins but could not. It plea-sed God to put it into the heart of one to ask him, *Whe-ther he had any Familiarity with the Devil*? he got out so much then as, *Yes*. He fetching Mr. *Pierson*, the Convulsion Fits left him, and he confessed all, how it had been with him. That very night the Devil came to him, and told him, *Had he blabbed out such things He would teach him to blabb*! and if he would not then Write and Seal the Agreement, he would tear him in pieces, and he refusing, the Devil took a corporal Pos-session of him, and hath not ceased to torment him ex-treamly ever since. If any thing be spoken to him, the Devil answereth (and many times he barks like a Fox and hisseth like a Serpent) sometimes with horrible Blasphemies against the Name of Christ; and at some o-ther times the Boy is sensible. When he hath the liberty of his Voice, he tells what the Devil saith to him, urging him to Seal the Covenant still, and that he will bring Paper, Pen and Ink in the night, whe

no

none ſhall ſee, pleading, that *God hath caſt him off*, *that Chriſt cannot ſave him*: That *when he was upon Earth, he could caſt out Devils, but now he is in Heaven he cannot*, Sometimes he is ready to yield to all in a deſperate way. Sometimes he breaks out into Confeſſion of his former ſins, as they come into his mind; exceedingly judging himſelf, and juſtifying GOD in his for ever leaving of him in the hands of Satan. Once he was heard to Pray in ſuch a manner ſo ſuteable to his Condition, ſo Aggravating his Sin, and pleading with God for mercy, and in ſuch a ſtrange, high, enlarged manner, as judicious godly perſons then preſent, affirm they never heard the like in their lives, that it drew abundance of tears from the eyes of all preſent, being about twenty perſons. But his torment increaſed upon him worſe after ſuch a time; or if any thing were ſpoken to him from the Word of God by others, or they pray with him. The laſt week after he had confeſſed one ſtrange Paſſage, namely that once in Diſcourſe he told the Devil, that if he would make his Spittle to ſcald a Dog, he would then go on in a way of *L*ying and Diſſembling, and believe that he ſhould do it, which he ſaid, he did with all his heart, and ſo ſpit on the Dog, and with that a deal of Scalding Water did pour on the Dog. In purſuance of his Promiſe, he went on in a way of Lying and Diſſembling: That when he was urged about it, that he had done ſome miſchief to the Dog, then he fell down into a Swound, as if he had been dead. As ſoon as he had confeſſed this, the Devil went out of him with an aſtoniſhing Noiſe, to the terrour of thoſe then preſent: and ſo he continued one day. The next day being much troubled in himſelf for one ſpecial Paſſage in his Diſcourſe with the Devil, when he appeared to him as a Fox; ſaith he to the Devil, *I have formerly ſought to God, and he hath been near unto me*: With that the Devil enraged, ſaid unto him then, *What, are you got hither?* and fell to Threatning of him. He ſaid to him again, *But I find no ſuch Thoughts now, but* *do and will believe you now more than the Word of God* which saith in Isa. 55. *Seek the Lord*, &c. and said further, *What comfort you shall afford me, I shall rely upon you for it.* Remembring this Passage the Devil appeared to him, ready to enter into him again. Thereby much astonished, having the Bible in his hand, he opened it, and, as it were of it self, at that place of *Isai.* 55. his Eye was fixed upon it, and his Conscience accusing him for abusing the Word a year ago, his heart failing him and the Devil entred into him again a second time, railing upon him, and calling him Blab-tongue, and Rogue! he had *promis'd to keep things secret, he would teach him to blabb, he would tear him in pieces.* Since, he hath kept his Body in continual Motion, speaking in him, and by him, with a formidable Voice: sometimes singing of Verses wicked and witty, that formerly he had made against his Father's Ministry, and the Word of God, &c. When the Boy is come to himself, they tell him of them, and he ownes them, that indeed such he did make. Mr. *Eaton* being his Uncle, sent a Letter to him, which he told of before it came, saying also, it would be goodly stuff! Jeering at him. By and by the Letter came in, and none of the people knew of it before. He speaks of men coming to him before they come in Sight: and once two being with him, their Backs turned, the Devil carried him away, they knew not how, and after search they found him in a Cellar, as dead, but after a little space he came to Life again. And another time, threw him up into a Chamber, stopped him up into a Hole, where they after found him. Another time he carried him about a Bow-Shot and threw him into a Hog-Stye amongst Swine, which ran away with a terrible noise.

Here is as much to be seen of the Venom of Sin, the Wrath of God against Sin, the Malice of the Devil, and yet his limited Power, and the Reasonings of Satan in an ocular Demonstration, as hath fallen out in any Age. Also the strange and high Expressions of a distressed Soul in a way of Judging himſelf and pleading for Mercy, ſuch as may be wondered at by all that hear of it; and more very obſervable Paſſages could not be written for want of Time, which will after appear.

Advertiſement.

Of what did after appear, I have no Account; but what did then appear, is ſo undoubted and ſo wonderful, that it will ſufficiently atone for my Publication of it.

EXAMPLE VI. and VII.

HAd there been Diligence enough uſed by them that have heard and ſeen amazing Inſtances of Witchcraft, our Number of Memorable Providences under this Head, had reached beyond the Perfect. However, before I have done Writing, I will inſert an Example or two, communicated unto me by a Gentleman of ſufficient Fidelity to make a Story of his Relating Credible. The Things were ſuch as happened in the Town whereof himſelf is Miniſter; and they are but ſome of more which he favoured me with the Communication of. But, it ſeems, I muſt be obliged, to conceal the Names of the Parties concerned, leſt ſome ſhould be Offended, tho' None could be Injured by the mention of them.

¶ In a Town which is none of the youngeſt in this Countrey, there dwelt a very Godly and Honeſt Man, who upon ſome Provocation, received very Angry and Threatning Expreſſions, from two Women in the Neighbourhood; ſoon upon this, diverſe of his Cattel in a ſtrange manner died; and the man himſelf ſometimes was haunted with ſights of the Women, as he thought, encountring of him. He grew indiſpoſed in his Body very unaccountably; and one day repaired unto a Church Meeting then held in that place, with a Reſolution there to declare what he had met withal. The man was one of ſuch Figure and Reſpect among them, that the Paſtor ſingled out him for to pray in the Aſſembly before their breaking up. He pray'd with a more than usual measure of both Devotion and Discretio but just as he was coming to that part of his Praye wherein he intended to Petition Heaven for the Disco very of Witchcrafts which had been among them, h sunk down Speechless and Senseless; and was by h Friends carried away to a Bed; where he lay for tw or three hours in horrible Distress, fearfully starting and staring and crying out *Lord, I am stabb'd*! and no looking whistly to and fro, he said, *O here are wick persons among us, even among US*; and he Complained *I came hither with a full purpose to tell what I knew, bu now* (said he) *I ly like a Fool!* Thus he continue until the Meeting was over, and then his Fits left him only he remained very sore. One or two more suc Fits he had after that; but afterwards a more pri vat sort of Torture was employ'd upon him. He wa advised by a worthy man to apply himself unto Magistrat; and warned, That he would shortly b Murdered, if he did not. He took not the Counsel; but languished for some Weeks; yet able to Walk an Work: but then, he had his Breath and Life sudden ly taken away from him, in a manner of which no full Account could be given.

The man had a Son invaded with the like Fits, bu God gave deliverance to him in answer to the Prayer of his people for him.

¶. In the same Town, there yet lives a very piou Woman, that from another Woman of ill Fame, recei ved a small gift, which was eaten by her. Upon th Eating of it, she became strangely altered and affli cted; and hindred from Sleeping at Night, by the Pull of some invisible Hand for a long while together. A Shape or two of, I know not who, likewise haunte her, and gave her no little Trouble. At last, a Fit ex traordinary violent came upon her; wherein she pointe her Hand, and fixed her Eye, much upon the Chimney and spake at a rate that astonished all about her. Anon she broke forth into Prayer, and yet could bring ou

scarce

scarce more than a Syllable at a time. In her short Prayer she grew up to an high Act of Faith, and said, (by Syllables, and with Stammerings) *Lord, Thou hast been my Hope, and in Thee will I put my Trust; Thou hast been my Salvation here, and wilt be so for ever and ever!* Upon which her Fit left her; and she afterwards grew very well; still remaining so.

¶ There were diverse other strange Things, which from the same Hand, I can both Relate and Believe, As, Of a Child bewitched into Lameness, and recovered immediatly, by a Terrour given to the vile Authoress of the Mischief; but the exact Print, Image and Colour of an Orange made on the Childs Leg, presently upon the sending of an Orange to the Witch by the Mother of the Child, who yet had no evil design in making of the Present. And of other Children, which a palpable Witchcraft made its Impressions on; but *Manum de Tabala.*

I entreat every Reader, to make such an Use of these things, as may promote his own wellfare, and advance the Glory of God; and so answer the Intent of the Writer, who,

Hac scribens studuit, bene de Pietate mereri.

There now remain two Discourses, for the Reader to be entertained with; the latter of which was delivered unto my own Congregation; on the Occasion of what befell *Goodwin*'s Children: but the former of them was deliver'd unto the same Congregation on the Occasion of a horrid Self-Murder committed by a Possessed Woman in the Neighbourhood. The Discourses were suited unto a Popular Auditory: but things that are not accurat may be profitable, if the Blessing of God accompany them.

A Dis-

A DISCOURSE on the POWER *and* MALICE *of the*

DEVILS

I *Pet.* V. 8.

--- *Your Adversary the Devil, as a Roaring Lion, walketh about, seeking whom he may devour.*

IT is a Relation made by *David* of an Encounter by him once met withal, in 1 *Sam.* 17. 34. *Thy Servant kept his Father's sheep, and there came a Lion, and took a Lamb out of the Flock.* There is an horrid Lion by which your Souls are pursued and endangered. This Lion fetch'd away, after a very dismal manner, one that was with us, when this Flock was last before the Lord; and he seeks, he longs, he roars, in that or some way to make a Prey of all. I am *keeping my Father's sheep*, and would labour to rescue from the Hellish Lion every Lamb that may ly in his way. Accept therefore the Text now read, as, *The warning of the Lord.*

Multitudes of Jews, dispersed in diverse Countries being Converted and Baptised by the Ministry of the Apostle *Peter*, at *Jerusalem*; he writes to them an excellent Epistle, to fortifie them against the Persecution which their Christianity might expose them to. He advises them, first, unto the more general, and then, unto the special Duties of the Christian Religion. The last of his Divine Counsels is, To *resist the temptations of the Devil.* And the Text before us contains the Argument whereby we are to be excited thereunto; 'tis drawn from the Disposition of the Devil; who is here exhibited, *First*, as an Adversary. *Secondly*, as a potent Adversary, a Lion. *Thirdly*, as a cruel Adversary, a roaring Lion. *Fourthly*, as a restless Adversary, a *Lion seeking whom he may devour.* This then is the Doctrine to be now attended unto.

The

The Devil is a potent, a cruel, and a restless Adversary to the Souls of Men.

Prop. 1. There is a Combination of Devils which our Air is fill'd withal. A Devil is a spiritual and a rational Substance, full of all Wickedness, confined by God unto our Air as his Goal, for his Apostacy from the Company and Employment of the Holy Angels. His Title is that in *Eph.* 6. 12. *a spiritual wickedness*; that is, a wicked spirit. A Devil was once an Angel, but Sin has brought him to be a Fallen Angel; an Angel full of Enmity to God and man; an Angel made a Prisoner within the Atmosphære of the Earth which we tread upon.

The Scriptures of Truth, allow us these Conclusions about the Devils of Hell.

We may first conclude, That the Devils are not meer Motions, or Qualities, or Distempers, as hath been by some absurdly enough conceived. The fond Sadducee derides the Doctrine of Devils, which we all embrace. But I pray, What things were those that *left their first estate*, being now *reserved in chains of darkness to the judgment of the great day*? What things be those that besought our Lord for liberty to *enter into the swine*? But we have among our selves lately seen plain Demonstrations, That there are Spirits, which understand, and argue, and will; and which are the enemies of all that is holy, and just, and Good.

We may secondly conclude, That these Devils are an Army in our Air. They are called in *Eph.* 2. 2. *the power* (or the Army) *of the Air.* There are diverse Miles of Air encompassing of this Terraqueous Globe; to that space it is that the Devils are limited, since their High-Treason against the God that made them. Here it is that they have a Play-house, as well as a Prison; here they play all their Devillish Pranks until the everlasting Fire shall begin to flame. Indeed, some Devils may keep more constantly to one Countrey, and some to another. Hence we read of some in *Marc.* 5. 10. *They besought our Lord*

Lord much, that he would not send them away out of th Countrey. But still the High-places of our air be th Receptacles of all the wicked Spirits.

We may conclude, Thirdly, That these Devils are a Army under a Leader too. There is a Government, Monarchy in the dark Regions; and hence in *Matt* 12. 24. we read about *Beelzebub*, the Prince of Devil There you have the Name of the Grand-Segniour who *King over the Children of Pride.* Probably, the Devils i their first Conspiracy and Rebellion against God, had notorious Ring-Leader; there was one of greater digni ty and influence than the rest, by whom they were hea ded; and they are all now under his Command. W have mention in the Sacred Oracles, of *the Devil and hi Angels.* This chief Devil called by way of eminency the Devil, but he has innumerable Slaves, and Officers and Emissaries, which are under an entire Subjection t him. His Orders they all observe; and therefore when we speak of the Devil, it includeth each privat Souldier as well as him that is principal Commander We say, The Devil, as we say, The Turk, or th Spaniard; it means any or every part of that infern Rendezvous. As it is said in *Ps.* 34. 6. *The Angel o the Lord encamps, i. e.* the whole Host of Angels are One in it.

Prop. 2. The Devils are the great Adversaries of hu mane Souls. 'Tis here said about the Devil, He is you Adversary; or as the Article intimats, he is that you Adversary.

If it be asked, How the Devils are our Adversaries In general they labour to do us all the mischief they can devise. They pursue our Hurt in all ways, an by all means. Yet in some sense they cannot come t us unless according to Law. Know, That the Greek word here notes properly an Adversary at Law; 'tis Law-Term that is used here. Thus first, the Devils an our Adversaries as Accusers. 'Tis the Character of th Devil in *Rev.* 12. 10. *The Accuser of our Brethren, whic*

accuset

accuseth *them before God day and night.* He is called a *Satan*, and a *Devil* for this very cause. The Devils are first our Tempters, and then our Accusers. They complain to God against us, that we do not fear Him, that we do not love Him, that we do not seek Him, as we ought to do: they represent our Faults before the Lord, as things that make us unfit for any mercy at His hands. There is a Court kept somewhere in the Invisible World, at which, Devils endeavour to prefer as many Complaints as they can against us. They first get, and then bring Matters of Accusation, which we might be Indicted and Condemned for.

2dly. The Devils are our Adversaries as Destroyers: they Plead and Pray as so many Attorneys, that a Judgment may be granted against us all; and then they Petition that they too, may be the Executioners of it. 'Tis illustrated in *Job*, 1. 11. and 2. 5. Satan urges upon God against *Job*, *put forth thine hand now, and touch his bone and his flesh.* They would fain have all manner of Miseries to be inflicted on us; and they try all they can, to gain Opportunities for doing their part, that we may be miserable. A Devil is called a destroying Angel. They are Devils usually, that are the Instruments of Divine Vengeance on the World. If it be asked, why the Devils are our Adversaries? There is a double Reason to be Assigned of it. One Reason of it is,

Their hatred of God. The Devils have shaken off the Law, and the Rule of God; and they cannot bear, that the Name of God should be acknowledged in the World. GOD and the Devils are sworn enemies to each other; and the Lord may say of them as in *Zech.* 11. 8 *My soul loathed them, and their soul also abhorred me.* Now the poor Children of men, both do the Service of God, and have the Image of God. We do the Service of God. Man is the Priest of the whole visible Creation. 'Tis by our Thoughts, 'tis by our Words, that all things else pay their Homage unto the Lord. The Devil that would be in the Throne of God, would ruine us, that

God

God may no more have the Honour of a Father, or th Fear of a Master in the world. *We* also have the Imag of God. In our Nature there is much, in our Vertu there is more of Gods Likeness. The Devil is a Tigre; they report of that wild Beast, it will tear the Pictur of a man, when it cannot reach the Person of a man There is a lively Shadow as it were, of God upon us and this the Tigres of Hell cannot endure.

A second Reason of it is, their Envy at man. The Devils behold man Exalted and Advanced above them selves. 'Tis said of the *Leviathan* in Job 41. 34. *He beholdeth all high things.* 'Tis fulfilled in the Pope also, and lastly in the Devil; he cannot brook it that any shoul be higher than himself. The Apostle intimats, that Prid was at first, *the Condemnation of the Devil.* 'Tis conjectured that the Devil being informed of Gods Decree, to hav a Man subsist in the Second Person of the Trinity; thi provoked him and his Accomplices to their Disobedience However, the Devil now sees Man saved, and himsel damned: Man in the Bosom of God, and himself in th Bottom of Hell: well, now thinks he, I will do this ma all the spite I can.

Prop. 3. The Devils are potent Adversaries of our souls.

The Devil is a Lion, and as it was said in Judg. 14 18. *What is stronger than a Lion?* He has a Power, an Interest, that may make us all to tremble at his Roaring. Hence we read in *Luke* 10 19. about *the power of the enemy:* and he is compared in *Cap.* 11. 21. unto *a strong Armed man.*

There be three things that show the power of our Adversaries.

First, The power of our Adversaries the Devils, lies in the nature of them. 'Tis said in Eph. 6. 12. *We fight not against flesh and blood only, but against principalities, and powers, and spiritual wickednesses.* They are Spiritual and therefore powerful. The Spirituality of the Devils enables them to strike us when we cannot see them; i makes them ready to attack us and surprise us at unspeak

abl

ble Disadvantages. The Devils are Spirits, and hence they count Iron but Straw, and Brass as rotten VVood; they are Spirits, and so they excel in strength; when they seem afraid of little Spels and Charms, it is only a stratagem by which they seek to decoy us into their dreadful power, more than before. One of them let loose, perhaps could slaughter an Army of an hundred thousand in a night.

Secondly, The power of our Adversaries the Devils, lies in the number of them. Even such little things as Mice, yea, and Lice, have proved horrible Plagues by becoming numerous. VVhat then may the Devils be, whose Troops amount unto many Legions? How many Devils can sometimes be spared, for the Vexation of one man? In the Bowels of one afflicted Child, I have heard that murmur made, *there are two or three of us!* Yea, we read in *Luke* 8. 30. of a Legion that kept a Garrison in one single person: a Legion contained twelve Thousand and five Hundred in it. Doubtless, there are far more Devils than there are men in the world. They swarm like the Frogs of *Egypt*, in every chamber of our houses. VVe can go, we can stir no where, but those wilde *Arabians* will be upon us.

Thirdly, The power of our Adversaries the Devils, lies in their Confederacies. The Devils are all as one among themselves; their Unity, their Agreement in their designs makes them formidable. VVe are told in Mat. 12. 26. *Satan is not divided against himself.* But more than so, the Devils have of their Party among our selves, yea, within our selves Devils have men on their side. All wicked men promote the ends of the Devils. 'Tis said, *The lusts of the Devil they will do.* 'Tis said, *The Devil works in the children of disobedience.* And the Devils have hearts on their side. Our wicked hearts will favour and humour the Devils in their Attempts, and betray us into their hands. When they made their Assault on our Saviour, 'tis said, *They found nothing in him.* But they find something in us, they find in us an In-mate, by whose

whose Treachery we become their Prey. This is the Power of the Enemy.

Prop 4. The Devils are also cruel Adversaries of our souls. The Devil is not only a Lion, but a Roaring, an Hungry, an angry Lion. Yea, according to that in *Rev.* 20. 2. he is not only a Lion, but a Dragon too. He will have no more mercy than a Lion, he will have no more mercy than a Dragon, upon all that comes in the way of his cruel Clutches. 'Twas the description of the *Chaldeans* in Hab. 1. 6. *That bitter and hasty nation*; to the Devils does it much more belong; they are a *Bitter and cruel nation.* Never was there such a merciless and a pitiless Tyrant, as the Devil is; nothing so much pleases that bloody Monster, as the Pain and the Death of our unhappy souls; and he has no Musick like the *groans of a deadly wounded man.* What a Prodigie of Cruelty was that *Roman* Emperour, who wished that *all his People had but one neck, that he might cut it off at a Blow*! Why The cruel Devil not only wished, but in Paradise he had and he did such an horrid thing. And it is he that Inspires vile men, with all the Cruelty that their Inquisitions and their Tortures give Example of.

Prop. 5. The Devils are likewise restless Adversaries of our souls: They go about, they are always in Action, always in Motion, that they may undo the souls of Men.

The Devil goes about. So could he say of himself in Job 1. 7. *I come from going to and fro in the earth, and from walking up and down in it.* This Prince goes his Progress, rides the Circuit through his whole Dominions, to see how his Work is carried on. And all that are under the Inspection of this Prime Visier, are continually travelling and labouring too, for the destruction of immortal souls. They go about, but how? We read in *Jude* 6. they are *kept in chains*; 'Tis by some rendered they are kept for Chains: but suppose them in Chains their Chains are so lengthened, and yet so limited, that they go about just where, and when, and how far the Permission

Permiſſion of God ſhall give them leave. As they are not now in all the Torment, ſo they are not now in al the Bondage intended for them. 'Twas the Sentence of wicked curſed *Cain* in *Gen.* 4. 14. *A fugitive and a vagabond ſhalt thou be upon the earth.*

'Tis the caſe of every Devil, he is a Fugitive and a Vagabond in our Air. [They go about] but why? For no good, you may be ſure. 'Tis with them as 'tis ſaid to be with their Vaſſals, in *Pſ.* 59.15: *They wander up and down for meat, and grudge if they be not ſatisfied.* They go about upon the Catch; they go about, that they may ſpy out Objects to work upon; they go about, with a raging appetite after Sin, and the Wages of it on the World. You ſhall ſee what the Poſtures and Methods of the Devil are; they are drawn with a Pencil of the Sanctuary, in Pſal. 10. 4. *He lies in wait ſecretly, as a Lion in his den; he lies in wait to catch the poor; he does catch the poor when he draws him into his net.* Such a deviliſh Adverſary have we to deal withal.

USE I. *Information.*

There are two Leſſons that we may learn from theſe things. We may ſay after the Apoſtle in 1 Joh. 3. 15. *In this the children of God are manifeſt, and the children of the Devil.*

Firſt. We may ſee from hence, who the Children of the Devil are; Roaring Lions that go about ſeeking whom they may devour; what are they, but the creatures whom the Devil is a Sire unto? We read of one in Ezek. 19.6. *Who became a young Lion and learned to catch the prey, and devoured men.* Such Lions there are often in the World; ſometimes there are men whoſe buſineſs, whoſe delight it is, to devour their Neighbours; men who go about to impair the Eſtate, who go about to blemiſh the Eſteem, who go about to debauch the ſouls of other men. What ſhal be ſaid of ſuch men? Alas, the Devil is the Father of them all, I have no Bleſſing for any of them; but yet I may ſay to them, *This is a lions whelp, to the prey, my ſon, thou art gone up.* This is juſt like the great old Lion; with him, even with him shall they one day be punished, and undergo the Doom in Jer. 51. 38. *They shall roar together like Lions, they shall yell as Lions whelps.* The great and the terrible GOD, will one day make the Sires and the Whelps together, to roar under the direful Impressions of His everlasting Wrath.

Secondly, From hence we may also see, who are the Children of God. 'Tis said of our Lord Jesus Christ, in Act. 10. 38. *He went about doing good.* There are some that go about seeking whom they may Instruct, that go about seeking whom they may Convert, that go about seeking whom they may Relieve. The *Lion of the tribe of Judah*, is a Father to these Holy men; not the Devil but the Saviour is their Pattern. The blessed, the glorious Angels, and not the outragious Devils, do thus improve themselves. Go on, Souls go on, thus to go about. I remember old Mr. *Latimer* in a Sermon, has that sharp Reflection upon the lazy Bishops of his time, that seldom or never preached in any one Pulpit of all their Diocess. *For shame (said he) you negligent Prelates, if you will not learn of God, and Christ, and good Men, then learn of the Devil, learn of the Devil, who is always at work in his* Diocess. Truly, we may learn of the Devil, to go about seeking the Welfare of those, whom he goes about seeking the Ruine of.

USE II. *Exhortation.*

We have two things now incumbent on us.

1. Let us *avoid* the *roaring Lion*, who *goes about seeking whom he may devour.* Let us not be willingly in the way of Devils, who are ever aiming at our Confusion.

First, Let us get from the Roaring Lion, by a sincere turning to God in Christ. Hear and quake all you that are yet in your unregenerate estate; you are in the mouth of the Roaring Lion: Oh, how can you be satisfied or contented there? In Conversion, we are told in *Act.* 26. 18 men are turned *from the power of satan unto God.* Man, thou art under the power of Satan, until thou art turning: O save thy self before it be too late. One once being ready to be devoured by a Lion, cry'd out, Help, help, I am yet alive! Help, I am yet alive! O thou art yet alive, but if thou art not quickly redeemed from the Lion, it will ere long be *All too late! All too late!* Quickly then renounce the service of the Devil; quickly loath, quickly leave all your sins; quickly run to God in Christ, and say unto Him, as in *Isa.* 26. 13. *O Lord our God, other lords besides Thee have had dominion over us, but now we will make mention of thy Name alone.*

Secondly, Let us keep from the Roaring Lion, by a sincere shunning of what will peculiarly bring us within his reach. Indeed every Lust as it were, surrenders us up unto the *Devil*: every time a man gratifies a Lust, a Devil is invited into the soul of that man; and by every new Act of it, he takes a new Hold of the soul. But some Vices there are, which give the Devils peculiar Opportunities to devour us: of these take heed with a more than ordinary Caution.

Particularly,

First. Beware of Discontent. The Devils are wonderfully discontented Spirits; and none more than discontented Persons, ly open to their Invasion and Annoyance. The discontented man is angry at God; it is a Rage at God, it is a Fret at God, which discomposes him. We are told about the man that is angry at his Neighbour, in *Eph.* 4. 27. *He gives place to the Devil.* How much more may this be said about the man who is angry at his Maker? The Devil finds a place in the soul of such a man. Be not angry at any Poverty, be not angry at any Calumny, be not angry at any Affliction whatsoever. Discontent opens the doors of the soul, for all the Devils of Hell to enter in.

2dly. Beware of Idleness. If thou art idle, know that the Devil is not so; the idle soul is an empty House; there happens to it that thing in Mat. 12. 44. *The unclean spirit walks to and fro, and comes and finds the house empty, then goeth he and taketh with himself seven other spirits, more wicked than himself, and they enter in.* When the Devil finds an Idle person, he as it were calls to more of his crue, Come here! come here! A brave prize, for us all! When was a *David* made a prize for a Devil? It was when he rose from his Couch in the Afternoon, and walked in his Balcony, as one that had nothing at all to do. Of Idleness comes no Goodness.

Thirdly, Beware of bad Company. That is, (I had almost said) the greatest engine the Devil has, to trepan the children of men withal. An evil Companion is Gin for a soul. The Devils will have thee fast enough, if thou walkest in the counsel of the ungodly, and standest in the way of Sinners, and sitest in the seat of the scornful. The Devils, nay, and the Gallows too, at length often devour those that bad Company shal seduce. 'Twas said to them of Old, *Depart from the tents of the wicked men, lest the earth swallow you up.* Even so, Depart from the Knots, depart from the Cups of wicked men, lest the Devil swallow you up. 'Tis said in Prov. 13. 20. *A companion of fools shall be destroyed.*

II. Let us Resist the Roaring Lion, who goes about seeking whom he may devour.

Do you find the Devil ready to devour you? Be you as ready to oppose him. It is mentioned as a sore calamity in *Psal.* 109. 6. *Let Satan stand at his right hand.* Alas! This is the condition of our Souls; we have Satan at hand, seeking to grip us in his hideous Claws.

How many Temptations does the Devil seek to devour your Souls withal? Temptations to Uncleanness and Wordliness are devouring of many. Temptations to Atheism and Blasphemy are devouring of others, Perhaps, Temptations to Self-Murder have near devoured some unhappy souls. O Remember whence all these Temptations do arise. These things are the Roarings of the Hellish Lion; and will you hearken to him? Is there any thing in these cursed Roarings to perswade your Hearkning thereunto? What Benefit, what Advantage, do you think these horrid Roarings can propound?

Com-

Come then, Resist the Temptations of this roaring Lion. 'Tis said in *Jam*, 4. 7. *Resist the devil, and he will flee from you.* If you fly, he will be a Lion, if you fight, he will be a Gnat before you.

Est Leo, si fugias; si stas, quasi musca recedit.

Your Encounters call for two Things.

One is your Watch. Hence 'tis here said, *Be vigilant, because your adversary the devil, as a roaring lion walketh about*, When it was cryed out unto the Champion of *Israel* in *Judg.* 16. 20. *The Philistines be upon thee, Sampson*; Then he awoke out of his sleep. Thus it may be exclaimed, The Lions are upon thee O soul. O how watchful, how wakeful should this cause thee to be. Be watchful against all the devices of the devil. Be watchful in every place, be watchful in every thing; be jealous alwais, Has not the devil now some design upon me?

The Second is your Faith. 'Tis recorded in *Heb.* 11. 33. *Some by Faith stopped the mouths of Lions.* Tho' thou shouldest be in a Den full of them, yet Faith, true Faith would muzzle them all. By Faith repair to Christ, who is the true *Sampson*, which meets and slayes the Lions that roar upon your souls. By Faith repair to the Rock even to the *Rock that is higher than I*! Where you may sit & shout and laugh at all the Lions that roar in the Wilderness, and say, *Where I am, there you cannot come.*

There are particularly two sorts of devouring Temptations, which I would couclude this Discourse with some suitable Reflections on.

*T*emptations to Atheism and Blasphemy, perhaps do molest some among us; possibly, *Terribilia de DEO*, and *Horribilia de Fide*; Diabolical Suggestions about our God and our Creed, may cast some of us into grievous Agonies: these things make many a good man to say, *I am weary of my life!* What shal in this case be done?

My Advice is,

*D*o not so much dispute, as deny the Injections of the wicked one. Don't give the devil so much honour as to argue and parley about his lewd proposals. Refuse them

presently

presently; refuse them peremptorily; so you silence them. When once an Atheistick or blasphemous Thought appears within your Minds, immediatly hiss it away, as the Priests did *Uzziah*, when they first saw the Leprosie in his Forehead. Let such Thoughts immediatly occasion in you, the savoury and gracious Thoughts that shall be Just contrary thereunto. If the Devil would have you think there is no God, then without any more ado, spite the Devil by such a Thought, with an Ejaculation contradicting of it, *Lord, I believe that thou art, and that thou art a Rewarder too.* Don't object, *What if there be no God?* But suppose for once, that God is. 'Tis by far the safer Supposal of the two. And then try whether to weary the Devil, be not the best way to Conquer him. Let every fiery Dart of Satan, fetch an holy Dart of Prayer and Grace from thee, and the Devil will soon be weary of his Methods.

Temptations to Self-Murder, may likewise be fierce upon some unhappy people here. 'Tis almost unaccountable, that at some times in some places here, melancholy distempered Ragings toward Self-Murder, have been in a manner Epidemical. And it would make ones hair stand, to see or hear what manifest Assistance the Devils have given to these unnatural Self-executions, when once they have been begun. 'Tis too evident, that persons are commonly bewitcht or possessed into these unreasonable Phrensies. But what shall these hurried people do?

My Advice is,

Don't conceal, much less obey the Motions of your Adversary. Failing in this, made a poor man after a faithful Sermon, in a neighbouring Town, presently to Drown himself in a Pit, that had not two Foot of Water in it. If you will not keep, that is the way not to take the Devils counsel. Let not him tye your Tongues, and it is likely he will not gain your Souls. Complain to a good God, of the Dangers in which you find your selves; cry to him, *Lord, I am oppressed, undertake for me* Complain also to a wise Friend. Let some prudent and

faithful

faithful Neighbour understand your Circumstances: 'tis possible, you may thereby escape the Snares with which the cruel Fowlers of Hell hope to trepan you into their dismal Clutches for evermore. Your Neighbours may do much for you, and may prove your Keepers if God shall please. It may be the unkindness of some Friend, may have thrown you into your present Madness? Now the kindness of some Friend may prove the antidote. Many times a natural Distemper, is that by which the Devil takes Advantage, to get the Souls of Self-Destroyers into his bloody hands. In this case for the tempted persons to disclose their Griefs, will be the way to obtain their Cures. Their Neighbours ought now to consult a skilful Physician for them; and oblige, yea, constrain them to follow his Directions. When the Humours on, and by which the Devil works, are taken away, perhaps he may be starved out of doors. Many times, again, the Sin of Slothfulness gives the Devil opportunity, to procure the Self-Destruction of the Sluggard. In this case too, the tempted person may be succoured by the Standers-by, becoming sensible of their Circumstances: their Neighbours may now compel them to follow their Business. A Calling, the Business of a Calling, is an Ordinance of God, sanctified by Him to deliver us from the evil Spirits, that enter into the empty House.

But most times, there may be some old and great Sin unrepented of, where Temptations to Self-Murder have a violence hardly to be with-stood. There was once a man among us, who in the horrours of Despair, uttered many dreadful Speeches against himself, and would often particularly say, I am all on a light Fire under the Wrath of God! This man yet never confessed any unusual sin, but this; that having gotten about Forty pounds by his Labour, he had spent it in wicked Company: but in his anguish of spirit he hanged himself. There was once a Woman among us, who under sickness, had made Vows of a new Life; but apprehending some

Defects

defects in her conversation afterward, she fell into the distraction wherein sh. also hanged her self. And the Sin of Adultery and Drunkenness has more than once issued in such a destructive Desperation. In case of this or any such Guilt, Confession with Repentance affords a present Remedy. To fly from Soul-terrour by Self-murder, is to leap out of the Frying-pan into the Fire. Poor tempted People, I must like *Paul* in prison, cry with a loud voice unto you, *Do your selves no harm*; all may be well yet, if you will hearken to the Counsels of the Lord.

Now, *Do thou, O God of peace, bruise Satan under our feet, world without end.* Amen.

A DISCOURSE on *WITCHCRAFT.*

I. Sam. XV. 23.
Rebellion is as the sin of witchcraft.

AS it is the Interest of all Christians to Consider the wondrous Works of God, so it is the Duty of all Ministers to study those of his VVords, with a peculiar Application, at which his VVorks like Hands in the Margin thereof do point, with Endeavours to make their Hearers understand what Lessons of the former the Voices of the latter do more especially direct unto.

A pious Family in this Town has lately had befalling of it, a Providence full of many Circumstances very astonishing; a Providence, wherein the power of GOD, the Success of Prayer, and the Existence with the Operation of Devils, has been demonstrated in a manner truly extraordinary; a Providence, whereof you have heard much, but I have seen more, and whereof neither you nor I can take a due Notice, without a solemn Discourse at this time upon it. 'Tis a Tribute owing to God that I Dispense,

spense, and 'tis a Revenge due unto Satan that you should attend the Truths proper to be delivered on an Occasion so Remarkable.

When some poor people fell into the hands of a *Pilate* our Saviour saw cause to preach a Sermon about Repentance thereupon: What less than a Sermon can be call'd for when some poor Children have lately fall'n into the hands of a Devil? tho' thanks be to our *David*, the Lambs are like to be delivered from the Hellish Monsters to which they were become a *Prey*. And this may seem the rather convenient, because the godly Father of the Children has desired it. For which cause the Text before us may be proper to be insisted on.

The Great GOD had three several times declared that the Nation of the *Amalekites* was to be destroyed and extirpated for evermore. King *Saul* was now employed with an Expedition against them, to accomplish that *Prediction*, and to execute the Vengeance of Heaven upon the present Generation of them, not only for their own Cruelty and Villany, but also for the Wickedness of their Ancestors four hundred years before. The Soveraign God had Anathematized every living thing among them, and ordered that both Man and Beast should fall in the day of slaughter. The Army, on I know not what pretence, did not observe this Commission, for which reason *Samuel* is now sent unto their Leader with dismal Rebukes and heavy Tidings for his Disobedience. In the Text before us, the *Prophet* aggravats the Sin of *Saul*.

1. By Describing of the Sin. The right Name is here put upon it; and it is called Rebellion against God.

2. By comparing of the Sin. It is resembled unto Witchcraft it self; not an Equality, but a Similitude between them is intended. It is not affirmed to be as great an Evil, but as true an Evil as Witchcraft is. That Witchcraft was a Sin far from venial, must be own'd by *Saul*, who had lately scow'red all the VVitches out of *Israel*: It is now said, Such a Fault is thine. The following Expression carries on the same sense;

and the meaning of that is, that they who adored a Idol, (for so I would rather translate the word here rendered Iniquity) or they who consulted a Teraphim which was a sort of a little Image from whence *Dæmons* gave Answers to Enquirers; even these are not more unquestionable Sinners, than those that add *Stubbornness* to Rebellion against the Lord.

But the Doctrine which we have now before us, is,

That VVitchcraft is a monstrous and an horrid Evil which yet all Rebellion against GOD may be too much compar'd unto.

By the ensuing Propositions, we may state and shape this Truth aright in our minds.

PROP. I.

Such an Hellish thing there is as *Witchcraft* in the world. There are two things which will be desired for the advantage of this Assertion. It should *first* be show'd,

VVhat *Witchcraft* is;

My Hearers will not expect from me an accurate Definition of the vile thing; since the grace of God has given me the Happiness to speak without Experience of it. But from Accounts both by Reading and Hearing I have learn'd to describe it so.

Witchcraft is the doing of strange (and for the most part ill) things by the help of evil Spirits Covenanting with (and usually Representing of) the woful Children of men.

This is the Diabolical Art that *Witches* are notorious for.

First; VVitches are the doers of strange things, they cannot indeed perform any proper Miracles; those are things to be done only by the Favourites and Embassadours of the LORD. But wonders are often produced by them, though chiefly such wonders as the Apostle calls in 2 Thes. 2. 9. Lying wonders. There are wonderful Storms in the great world, and wonderful wounds in the little world, often effected by

these

ese evil Causes. They do things which transcend the rdinary course of Nature, and which puzzle the ordinary sense of Mankind. Some strange things are done by em in a way of real Production. They do really torment ey do really afflict those that their Spite shal extend un-o. Other strange things are done by them in a way of rafty Illusion. They do craftily make of the Air, the Fi-ures and Colours of things that never can be truly creat-d by them. All men might see, but I believe, no man ould feel some of the things which the Magicians of E-pt, exhibited of old.

Secondly, They are not only strange things, but ill things, at witches are the doers of. In this regard also they are ot the Authors of Miracles: those are things commonly one for the good of Man, always done for the praise of od But of these Hell-hounds it may in a special manner e said, as in *Psal.* 52.3. *Thou lovest evil more than good.* For e most part they labour to Rob Man of his Ease or his ealth; they labour to wrong God of his Glory. There is ention of Creatures that they call white VVitches, which o only good Turns for their Neighbours. I suspect that ere are none of that sort; but rather think, *There is none at doeth good, no, not one.* If they do good, it is only that ey may do hurt.

Thirdly, It is by virtue of evil Spirits that VVitches o what they do. VVe read in *Ephes* 2 2. about the *rince of the power of the Air.* There is confined unto the tmosphere of our Air a vast power, or Army of Evil pirits, under the Government of a Prince who employs em in a continual Opposition to the Designs of GOD: he Name of that Leviathan who is the Grand Seigniour f Hell, we find in the Scripture to be *Beelzebub.* Under e Command of that mighty Tyrant there are vast Legi-ns & Myriads of *Devils*, whose Businesses and Accomplish-ents are not all the same. Every one has his *Post*, and is work; and they are all glad of an opportunity to e mischievous in the World. These are they by whom Witches do exert their Devilish and malign Rage upon their Neighbours: And especially Two A concur hereunto: The First is, their Covenanting w the VVitches. *There* is a most hellish League made tween them, with various Rites and Ceremonies. T VVitches promise to serve the Devils, and the *Devils* pr mise to help the VVitches; How? It is not convenient be related. *The* second is, Their Representing of t VVitches. And hereby indeed these are drawn into snar and cords of Death. *The* devils, when they go upon t Errands of the VVitches, do bear their Names; a hence do *Harmes* to come to be carried from the Devi to the VVitches. VVe need not suppose such a wi thing as the *Transforming* of those VVitches into Bru or Birds, as we too often do.

It should next be proved, that VVitchcraft is.

The Beeing of such a thing is denied by many th place a great part of their smal wit in reading the St ries that are told of it. *Their* chief Argument is, th they never saw any VVitches, therefore there are non Just as if you or I should say, we never met with any Ro bers on the Road, therefore there never was any Pa ding there.

Indeed the Devils are loath to have true Notions VVitches entertained with us. I have beheld them to p out the eyes of an enchanted Child, when a Book th proves, There is VVitchcraft, was laid before her B there are especially two Demonstrations that evince t Being of that Infernal mysterious thing.

First, *We* have the testimony of Scripture for i *VV*e find *VV*itchcrafts often mentioned, sometime, b way of Assertion, sometimes by way of Allusion, in th Oracles of God Besides that, we have there the Histo of diverse *VV*itches in these infallible and inspire writings Particularly, the Instance of the *VV*itch at *End* in 1 *Sam.* 28. is so plain and full that *VV*itch craft it self is not a more amazing thing, than a Dispute about the Beeing of it, after this. *The* Advoca

Witches must use more Tricks to make Nonsense of [th]e Bible, than ever the witch of Endor used in her Ma[gi]cal Incantations, if they would evade the Force of [th]at famous History. They that believe no witches, do [im]agine that Jugglers only are meant by them whom the [Sa]cred Writ calleth so. But what do they think of [th]at Law in *Exod.* 22. 18. *Thou shalt not suffer a witch to [liv]e?* Methinks 'tis a little too hard to punish every silly [Ju]*ggler* with so great Severity.

Secondly, We have the *Testimony of Experience for it.* What will those *Incredulous*, who must be the only *In[ge]nious* men say to this? Many VVitches have like those [in] *Act.* 19. 18. *Confessed and shewed their Deeds.* VVe [se]e those things done, that it is impossible any *Disease*, [o]r any *Deceit* should procure. VVe see some hideous [W]*retches* in hideous *Horrours* confessing, *That they did the [M]ischiefs.* This Confession is often made by them that [a]re owners of as much Reason as the people that laugh [at] all *Conceit of Witchcraft*: the exactest Scrutiny of [sk]ilful Physicians cannot find any distraction in their [m]inds. This *Confession* is often made by them that are [ap]art One from another, and yet they agree in all the [C]ircumstances of it. This *Confession* is often made by [the]m that at the same time will produce the *Engines and [En]signs of their Hellish Trade*, and give the standers-by [an] *Occular Conviction of what they do*, and how. There [ca]n be no Judgment left of any *Humane affairs*, if such [Co]nfessions must be Ridiculed: all the *Murders*, yea, and [al]l the *Bargains* in the world must be meer *Imagination* [if] such *Confessions* are of no Account.

PROP. II.

[W]VVITCHCRAFT is a most Monstrous and Hor[ri]d Evil. Indeed there is a vast heap of bloody roar[in]g Impieties contained in the Bowels of it. VVitch[cr]aft is a Renouncing of GOD, and Advancing of a [fil]thy *Devil* into the Throne of the Most High; 'tis [th]e most nefandous *High Treason* against the Majesty [on] High. VVitchcraft, is a Renouncing of *Christ*, and

 preferring

preferring the Communion of a loathsome lying Devil before all the Salvation of the Lord Redeemer; tis a Trampling under foot that Blood which is more precious than Hills of Silver, or whole Mountains of Gold. There is in Witchcraft, a most explicite Renouncing of all that is holy and just and good. The Law given by God the Prayer taught by Christ, the Creed left by the Apostles is become abominable where Witchcraft is embraced. The very Reciting of those blessed things is commonly burdensome where Witchcraft is. All the sure Mercies of the new Covenant, and all the just Duties of it, are utterly abdicated by that cursed Covenant which Witchcraft is constituted with. Witchcraft is a Siding with Hell against Heaven and Earth; and therefore a Witch is not to be endured in either of them. 'Tis a Capital Crime and it is to be prosecuted as a piece of Devilism that would not only deprive God and Christ of all his Honour, but also plunder man of all his Comfort. *Witchcraft* it's an impotent, but an impudent Essay to make Hell of the Universe, and to allow nothing but a *Tophet* in the World. *Witchcraft*,--- What shal I say of it! It is the furthest Effort of our Original Sin; and all that can make any Practice or Person odious, is here in the Exaltation of it.

It was the speech of *Jehu* to *Joram*, in 2 *King.* 9. 22. *What peace, so long as the Witchcrafts of thy mother are so many?* Truly, as *Witchcraft* would break the peace of all Mankind, so 'tis a thing that should enjoy no Peace among the Children of *Adam.* Nothing too vile can be said of, nothing too hard can be done to such an horrible iniquity as *Witchcraft* is.

PROP. III.

Rebellion against God has very much like to Witchcraft in it. Something like to Witchcraft there is in an Act of Rebellion; But a Course of Rebellion has much more like to *Witchcraft* in it. Some persons there are whose way is that of wickedness, whose work is that of *Iniquity*. Those persons do *what is like Witchcraft* every day

day. For, First, In Rebellion, men cast off the Authority of GOD: The Witch declares a Will to be no more disposed and ordered by the Will of God; she says, *God shall not be my Governour*. Such is the Language of Rebellion. When men rebel against God. They say like him in Exod. 5. 2. *I know not the Lord, and I will not obey his voice.* They say like them in Jer. 44. 16. *As for the word spoken in the Name of the Lord, we will not hearken thereunto.* There is indeed a sort of Atheism in Rebellion. The Sinner is a Fool that wishes, *O that there were no God!* that resolves, *God shall not be Lord over me.*

Secondly, In Rebellion men refuse the Salvation of Christ. The Witch contemns all the offers of the Gospel, and prizes the dirty proffers that Satan makes before them all. This is the plain English of Rebellion; it says What is tendered by the Devil, is better than what is tendered by the Saviour. The LORD said about *Israel* of old in Psal. 81. 11. *Israel would none of Me.* Thus 'tis when men rebel against God. A Jesus may say, *Those poor creatures will have none of me, nor of my Blood.* A Pardon may say, *Those guilty creatures will have none of me.* A Kingdom may say, *Those undone creatures will have none of me.* Where Sin is committed, there Christ is despised. This doleful Phrensy is in all Rebellion against the Lord.

Thirdly, In Rebellion men choose and serve the Devil as their Lord. The VVitch makes an horrible Agreement with Devils, to be theirs alone. This is the intent of all Rebellion too. It in short says, Let the Devil rule; it says, Let the Devil be humoured and gratified. As that cowardly King said unto the *Syrian*, 1 King. 20. 4. *My Lord, O King, I am thine, and all that I have.* Thus the ungodly man says unto the Devil; Thou art my Lord and my King. All Rebellion against God is in Obedience to the Devil When men rebel, they lay their wit, their love, their strength, and all the Instuments of that Rebellion before the Devil, and they say, This

is

is thine, O Satan, and all that they have. They do even sell themselves to the Devil! as we read of one, *he sold himself to work wickedness.*

Fourthly, In Rebellion, Men cast the Bond and the good of their Baptism behind their back. Among the customs of Witches, this is one. They Renounce their Baptism in a manner very Diabolical. The same thing is done in the Rebellion of a wicked man. We are told in 1 *Pet.* 3. 21. that the thing which renders Baptism available is *The answer of a good Conscience.* But in Rebellion against God, men give the answer of an Evil Conscience, and so make a Nullity of their Sacred Baptism. The Demand of God is, *Wilt thou believe as baptized persons do profess to do?* The Rebel answers, *No, I will continue shut up in my unbelief.* The demand of God is, *Wilt thou put on Christ, as the Baptized profess to do?* The Rebel answers, No, *I will put on the old man.* The Almighty God puts that Question, *wilt thou forsake the World, the Flesh, and the Devil*, as thy Baptism does oblige to do? In Rebellion the answer of sinful man is, No, *I will serve them all; they shall all be the Idols of my Soul.* With what Conscience can they answer so! But thus their Baptism is nothing with them.

Fifthly, All that rebel against God, are very mischievous in doing so. They are mischiefs that Witches are delighted in. Thus 'tis the end of Rebellion to bring destruction upon all that are near unto it. 'Tis said in *Eccles.* 9. 18. *One sinner destroyeth much good.* It is the ill hap of Sinners like Witches to do hurt wherever they come; they hurt the Souls of their Neighbours by the venom of their evil Communication; they hurt the Names of their Neighbours by their slanderous Defamation; they hurt their Estates by bringing down the fiery Judgments of Heaven upon all the Neighbour-hood. Unto Rebellion against God, are owing all the Distresses and Miseries of a calamitous world. This is the *Achan*, this is the troubler of us all.

The Improvement of these things now calls for our Earnest

earnest Heed; and unto each of our three Propositions, we may annex Applications agreeable thereunto.

I begin with the Use of the first Proposition.

1. By way of Information.

There are especially two Inferences to be drawn from this Position, That such a thing there is, as *Witchcraft* in the VVorld.

[First.] Since there are *Witches*, we are to suppose that there are Devils too: Those are the Objects that *Witches* converse withal. It was the Heresie of the ancient Sadducees in *Act.* 23. 8. The Sadducees do say, that there is neither Angel nor Spirit. And there are multitudes of Sadducees yet in our days; Fools, that say, seeing is Believing; and will believe nothing but what they see. A Devil, is in the Apprehension of those mighty acute Philosophers, no more than a Quality, or a Distemper. But, as Paul said unto Him of old, *King* Agrippa, *Believest thou the Prophets?* Thus I would say, Friend, *Believest thou the Scriptures?* I pray, VVhat sort of things were they, of whom we read in Jude 6. *Angels that kept not their first estate, but left their own Habitation, and be reserved in chains unto the judgement of the great day.* VVhat sort of things were they, who in *Matth.* 18. 16. *Besought* our Lord, *If thou cast us out, suffer us to go into the herd of swine?* VVhat thing was that, which in *Luk.* 4. 33. cryed out unto the Lord Jesus with a loud voice, *Let us alone?* Surely, these things could be none but Spiritual and rational Substances, full of all VVickedness against God, and Enmity against man. VVe shall come to have no Christ, but a Light within, and no Heaven, but a Frame of mind, if the Scriptures must be expounded after the Rules of the modern Sadducees. Perhaps though the Scriptures are Fables to that sort of men: Come then thou Sadducee, VVhat kind of thing is that which will so handle towardly ingenuous well-disposed persons? That if any Devotions be performed, they shall roar and tear unreasonably, and have such Noises & such Tortures in in them, as not only to hinder themselves wholly, but others too much from joyning in the Service; and strive to kick or strike the Minister in his Prayers, but have their hands or feet strangely stopt, when they are just come at him, and yet be quiet before and after the Worship? That if any idle or useless Discourse be going, they shall be well; but at any serious Discourse, they shall be tormented in all their Limbs. That if a Portion of the Bible be read, though they see and hear nothing of it, and though it may be in *Greek* or *Hebrew* too, they shall fall into terrible Agonies, which will be over when the Bible is laid aside. That they shall be able to peruse whole Pages of Evil-Books, but scarce a Line of a good one. That they shall Move and Fly, and tell secret things, as no ordinary Mortals can. Let me ask, *Is not the hand of* Joab *in all this?* Or is there not a Devil, whose Agency must account for things that are so extravagant? I am now to tell you, *That these eyes of mine have beheld all these things*, and many other more no less amazing. Christian, there are Devils; and soo many of them too, as sometimes a Legion of them are spar'd for the Vexation of one man. The Air in which we breath is full of them. Be sensible of this, you that obey God: there are Troops of Tempters on every side of thee. Awake, O soul, Awake, those Philistines of Hell are upon thee. Upon the least Affrightment in the dark, many simple people in the dark, many simple people cry out, *the Devil! the Devil!* Alas, there are Devils thronging about thee every day. O let the thought of it make thee a careful and a watchful man. And be sensible of this you that commit Sin, the Lord Jesus hath said of you, *Ye will do the lusts of your father the Devil.* How often do many of you, make a Mock and a Jeer of the Devil, while you are drudging for him? But know, that there are dreadful Devils to seize upon thy forlorn forsaken soul, at its departure hence. O become a new man at the thought of this.

2. Since

2. Since there are Witches and Devils, we may conclude that there are also Immortal Souls. Devils would never contract with Withches for their Souls, if there were no such things to become a *Prey* unto them. One of the *Popes* when he lay dying said, *I shall now quickly know whether I have an Immortal Soul or not.* Within less than a hundred years, you and I shall be convinced of it, if we are not so before. We may truly say, Devils and Witches bear a witness against them that have any scruple of it. There are some dreaming Hereticks, that hold Man wholly mortal. I am sure the Apostle *Paul* was not of their beastly Opinion, when he said in Phil. 1. 21. *I desire to be dissolved and to be with Christ.* Nor was the Martyr *Stephen* of their Opinion, when he expired saying, in Act. 7. 59 *Lord Jesus receive my spirit.* Nor was our Lord Jesus himself of that Opinion, when He said unto the Thief on the Cross, in Luk. 23. 43. *This day thou shalt be with me in Paradise.* 'Tis an Opinion unworthy of a man that is owner of a Soul. The mistaken *Indians*, when first they saw a man on Horseback, did conceit the Man and the Horse to be one Creature: it is as foul an Error, to conceit that it is but one thing which man consisteth of. No, 'Tis a right Anatomy of man, in Gen. 2. 7. *The Lord God formed man out of the dust of the ground, and breathed into his nostrils the breath of life, and man became a living Soul.* Remember, thou hast in thee a living Soul, or a Spirit, able to Know, and VVill, and Argue so, as nothing else in the visible Creation can. This living Soul is the Candle of the Lord within thee, and no VVind, no Death can ever extinguish it. O make much of this living Soul, save it, and do not sell it: it is a Jewel too precious to be thrown away. Do not sell thy soul for a song; take heed that the Devils make it not theirs by any Follies of thine.

2. *By way of Exhortation.*

There is one thing to be now pressed upon us all.

Let us wisely endeavour to be preserved from the Molestations

Molestations of all VVitchcraft whatsoever. Since there is a thing so dangerous, defend your selves, and shelter your selves by all right means, against the Annoyance of it.

Consider the multitudes of them, whom Witchcraft hath sometimes given Trouble to. Persons of all sorts, have been racked and ruined by it; and not a few of them neither. It is hardly twenty years ago, that a whole Kingdom in *Europe*, was alarm'd by such potent Witchcrafts, that some hundreds of poor Children were invaded with them. Persons of great Honour have sometimes been cruelly bewitched. What lately befell a worthy Knight in *Scotland*, is well known unto the VVorld. Persons of great Vertue too, have been bewitched, even into their Graves. But four years are passed, since a holy man was kill'd in this doleful way, after the Joy as well as the Grace of GOD, had been wonderfully filling of him. This Consideration should keep us from Censuring of those, that VVitchcraft may give Disturbance to: but it should put us on studying of our own Security. *Suppose ye that the enchanted Family in the Town, were sinners above all the Town, because they have suffered such things? I tell ye Nay, but except ye repent, ye may all be so dealt withal.* The Father of Lies uttered an awful Truth, when he said through the mouth of a possessed man, If God would give me leave, I would find enough in the best of you all, to make you all mine.

Consider also the Misery of them, whom VVitchcraft may be let loose upon. If *David* thought it a sad thing to fall into the hands of men; VVhat is it to fall into the hands of Devils? The hands of *Turks*, of *Spaniards*, of *Indians*, are not so dreadful as those hands that *witch*-do their works of Darkness by. O what a direful thing is it, to be prick't with Pins, and stabb'd with Knives all over, and to be fill'd all over with broken Bones? 'Tis impossible to reckon up the varieties of Miseries which those Monsters inflict, where they can have a Blow. No less than Death, and that a languishing and a terrible

terrible Death will satisfie the Rage of those formidable Dragons. Indeed Witchcraft sometimes grows up into Possession it self: the Devils that are permitted to tor- at last do possess the Bodies of the bewitched Sufferers; But who can bear the thoughts of that? who can forbear crying out, *O Lord, my flesh trembles for fear of thee, and I am afraid of thy judgments.*

What shall then be done for our Preservation? Away with all superstitious Preservatives: about those Confidences the Word of God is that, in Jer. 2. 37. *Thou shalt not prosper in them.*

But there are three admirable Amulets that I can heartily recommend unto you all.

The first preservative is, a fervent Prayer. Pour out that Prayer before the Lord, in Psal. 59. 2, 3. *Deliver me from the workers of iniquity, and save me from the bloody ones; for lo, they lie in wait for my soul.* And be much in Prayer every day. The Devils are afraid of our Prayers; they tremble and complain, and are in a sort of Anguish while our Prayers are going. There was a house of a renowned Minister in *France*, infested with evil Spirits; who though they had been very troublesome, yet when the good man was betaking himself to Prayer, they would say, *Now you are going to Prayer, I'le be gone.* Let us pray much, and we need fear nothing. Particularly, Let Ejaculatory Prayers be almost continually in our minds, and so we shall never ly open to the fiery darts of the wicked one.

The second Preservative is a lively Faith. The *Psalmist* well said, in Psal. 56. 2, 3. *Mine enemies would dayly swallow me up; At what time I am afraid, I will trust in thee.* Be not afraid of any Devils; if you are, turn the Fear into Faith. By Faith resign your selves to the Custody of Him that is the Keeper of *Israel.* By Faith perswade your selves, that He is able to keep what you have committed unto Him. Thus, run to the Rock, and there triumph over all the *powers of darkness.* Triumph and say, *The Lord is on my side; I will not fear: What can Hell do unto me?*

The third *Preservative* is, a Holy Life. There was a very Holy Man of old, *a man that feared God and eschewed evil*; and the Devils murmur'd in *Job.* 1. 10. *God has made an hedge about him.* The same have the Devils confest, when they have plotted against other Holy Men. Do not thou break the Hedge of God's Commandment, and perhaps he will not let any break the Hedge of His Providence, by which thou art secured. The Holy Angels are the Friends, the Guardians, the Companions, of all Holy Men; they may open their eyes, and see more with them than against them. A Camp, an Host of Angels, will fight against all the Harpies of Hell, which may offer to devour a Saint of GOD.

Use these things as the Shields of the Lord; so you shall be preserved in Christ Jesus, from the Assaults of the Destroyer. Suppose now that any VVitches may let fly their Curses at you, you are now like a Bird on the VVing in such Heaven ward Motions, that they cannot hitt you. Now the Devils and their Creatures, cannot say of you as the *Dæmon* said of the Christian woman, whom at a Stage-*Play* he took possession of, and being asked, gave this reason of his taking her, *I found her on my own ground.*

VVe pass on to the

USE of the *Second Proposition*;

And that must be a Counsel from God unto us all.

Particularly,

Since *Witchcraft* is an *Evil* so horrible.

1. To them that may be Enticed unto the Sin of VVitchcraft. To them we say,

1. Take heed that you be not by any Temptation, drawn into this monstrous and horrid *Evil.*

The best man that ever breathed, was tempted hereunto; that man who was more than a meer Man, was assaulted by the chief Devil of the lowest Hell with this Temptation, in *Mat.* 4. 9. *Fall down and worship me.* But by the *Sword of the Spi*[illegible] [illegible] shoot him off,

If any of you are by any Devil so sollicited, thus resist, thus repel all the Motions of the wicked one. Don't give your selves away to those Deceivers that will become Tormentors of your souls in another World.

It may be the proposal of this Counsel, may make some to say as he 2 King. 8. 13. *What? Is thy servant a dog, that he should do this great thing?* I answer, Alas, we should every one of us be a Dog and a Witch too, if God should leave us to our selves. It is the meer Grace of God, the Chains of which restrain us from bringing the Chains of Darkness upon our Souls. The humble and (therefore) Holy Martyr *Bradford*, when he heard of any Wickedness committed in the Neighbourhood, would lay his hand on his Breast and say, *In this heart of mine, is that which would render me as wicked as the worst in the world, if God should leave me to my self.* When we see a forlorn wretch executed for Witchcraft, you and I may say the same. They that are Witches now, once little dream't of ever becoming so. *Let him that stands, take heed lest he fall.* If we would not fall into that horrible Pit, let us follow these Directions.

Direction 1.

Avoid those ill Frames which are a Step to Witchcraft. There are especially two ill Frames which do lead people on to the worst VVitchcraft in the world. Shun a Frame of Discontent. VVhen persons are discontented with their own state; when persons through Discontent at their Poverty, or at their Misery, shall be always murmuring and repining at the Providence of God, the Devils do then invite them to an Agreement with, and a Relyance on them for help; downright VVitchcraft is the up-shot of it. VVe find in *Luk.* 4. 2. our Lord hungred, and then the Devil came in an audible or a visible manner to Him, though he had been more spiritually long before assaulting of Him. They are needy persons whom Devils make the most likely attempts upon. And some persons are not only Hungry

gry, but Angry too; but then every Fret, every Fume is as it were a Call to the Devils; it calls to them, com and help me. *Shun* also a Frame of ill-wishing. Ther is a Witchcraft begun in the Imprecations of wicke people. Many profane persons will wish the Devil t take this and that, or the Devil to do this and that and when they call, at last he comes; or at least th Devil does what they wish. Observe this, we are b our sins, worthy to have Mischiefs befalling us ever day; and the Devils are always ready to inflict wha we deserve. I am also apt to think, that the Devil are seldom able to hurt us in any of our exteriour Con cerns, without a Commission from some of our Fellow worms. It is intimated in *Gen*. 4. 9. That ever man is his *Brothers Keeper*: We are by our good wishe to keep our Brethren from the In-roads of Ill-spirit But when foul-mouth'd men shall wish Harm unto thei Neighbours, they give a Commission unto the Devils to perform what they desire; and if God should no mercifully prevent it, they would go thorow with i Hear this, you that in wild Passions will give every thin to the Devil: Hear it, you that will speak a Rot; a Pox and a Plague upon all that shall provoke you. I her Indict you as guilty of hellish Witchcraft in the sight o God. 'Tis the little Wapping of small Dogs, that stir up the cruel Mastives to fall upon the Sheep in th Field.

Direction 2.

Avoid all those ill Charms which are a piece of Witch-craft. The Devils have pretty Rattles, as well as fier Arrows: they that use the Rattles, will come at lengt to use the Arrows too. Do not play on the Brink o the Pit, lest you tumble in. It was complained in King. 17. 9. *The Children of Israel did secretly those thing that are not right against the Lord their God*. Even so i may be said, that the people among us do often an frequently those things that have a sort of Witchcraf in them.

Ther

There are manifold Sorceries practised among them that make a profession of Christianity, against which I would this day bear a witness in the Name of the most Holy Lord.

First, There are some that make use of wicked Charms for the curing of Mischiefs. It is too common a thing for persons to oppose Witchcrafts it self with Witchcraft. When they suppose one to be bewitched, they do with Burnings, and Bottles, and Horshoes, and, I know not what, magical Ceremonies endeavour his Relief. Mark what I say: To use any Remedy, the force of which depends upon the Compact of the Devils with the Witches, is to involve ones self in the cursed Compact: it is, as it were, to say, *O Devil, Thou hast agreed with such a person, that they shall be expos'd unto Torments by the use of such or such a Ceremony, we do now use the Ceremony, and expect thy blessing upon it.* This is the Language foamed out by this foolish Magick. Does not thy Conscience tremble at such Iniquity and Impiety? This may be to heal a Body, but it is to destroy a Soul. These persons give themselves to the Devils to be deliver'd from the Witches. And the people that are eas'd and helped by such means, they say, do usually come to unhappy Ends. Let me say as in 2 *Kings* 1. 3. *Is there not a God in Israel, that you go to Beelzebub?* What? will not Prayer and Faith do, but must the Black Art be used against our Enemies?

It is likewise too common a thing in almost every Disease to seek an unlawful Medicine. Thus for the Ague, for the Tooth-ach, and for what not? a mumbling of some words must be made, or a Paper of some words must be worn. From what can the Efficacy of these words proceed, but from the Consent and the Action of the Devils? The Witches have their Watch-words, which I list not to recite: upon those Watch-words the Devils do their Commands: These kinds of Spells are Watch-words to the Devils; and when a man has any Benefit by them, he cannot say as in *Psal.* 103. 3.

Bless the Lord, O my soul, who healeth all thy diseases. Man, First leave off the name of a Christian, before thou dost thus make thy self a Conjurer. I hope the Churches of the Lord Jesus will not bear it, that any in their Communion, should have this *Fellowship with the unfruitful works of darkness*. But this is not all; *Turn we yet again, and we shall see greater abominations*. For,

Secondly, There are some that make use of wicked Charms, for the finding of Secrets. The Lord hath told us, in *Deut.* 29. 29. *Secret things belong to God.* But these impious people must needs have a Taste of them. They will ask the Devils to inform their minds, and remove their doubts. This is the Witchcraft of them, that with a Sieve, or a Key will go to discover how their lost Goods are disposed of. This is the Witchcraft of them that with Glasses and Basons will go to discover how they shall be Related before they die. They are a sort of VVitches that thus employ themselves. And this is the VVitchcraft of the Judicial Astrologer. That Astrologer is a Cousin-German to a Conjurer. I think I know his Rules, and I am satisfied that his Judgment must at last be determined by his Impulse, or it is not worth an hundredth part of what the silly Enquirer pays him for it: and from whom, from what shall that Impulse come? Behold the Energy of Devils in it. It is likewise a sort of Sorcery, for persons to let their Bibles fall open, on purpose to determine what the state of their Souls is, from the first word they light upon. And some among us, they say, are so extreamly sinful, as to consult one whom they count a Conjurer, when they would understand what they know not otherwise. 'Tis horrible, that in this Land of Uprightness there should be any such Prank of VVickedness. I do earnestly testifie unto you, that these things are abominable: the voice of our God is, *O do them not, my soul hates them.* I do warn and charge you, Shun these execrable things, lest you be left unto the

the furthest Witchcraft committed by the abhorred of the Lord.

2. Take heed that you do not wrongfully accuse any other person, of this horrid and monstruous evil. It is the Character of a Godly man, in *Psal.* 15. 3. *He taketh not up a Reproach against his Neighbour.* What more dirty Reproach than that of Witchcraft can there be? Yet it is most readily cast upon worthy persons, when there is hardly a shadow of any reason for it. An ill look, or a cross word will make a Witch with many people who may on more ground be counted so themselves. There has been a fearful deal of Injury done in this way in this Town, to the good Name of the most credible persons in it. Persons of more Goodness and Esteem than any of their calumnious Abusers have been defamed for Witches about this Countrey, A Countrey full of lies. I beseech you, Let all Back-biting, and all Evil-surmising be put away from among you: do not, on small grounds Fly-blow the precious ointment of the good Name that thy Neighbour should have. On the least provocation, *I will never believe but such an one is a Witch* ----- that is presently the Sentence of some that might speak more warily than so. Alas, thou mightest with as much Honesty break open the House, or take away the Purse of thy Neighbour: His good Name is of more Account. They that indulge themselves in this course of Evil-judging, are usually pay'd home for it before they die; the just God sues them in an Action of Defamation, and makes their Names to be up too, before they leave the world.

Wee'l suppose the most probable Presumptions:

Suppose that a Person bewitched should pretend to see the Apparition of such and such an one, yet this may be no infallible Argument of their being Naughty People. It seems possible that the Devils may so traduce the most Innocent, the most Praiseworthy. Why may not spiritual Devils, as well as

Devils Incarnat get leave to do it? There was at *Groton* a while since, a very memorable Instance of such a thing; and what should hinder them that can imitate the Angels of Light, but that they may likewise personate the Children of Light, in their Delusions.

2. To them that have been seduced into the Sin of Witchcraft. And under this Rank, there are two sorts of persons to be addressed unto.

First, Let them that have been guilty of Implicit Witchcraft, now repent of their monstruous and horrid evil in it. I fear that I speak to some Scores, that may lay their hands on their mouths, and cry, Guilty, Guilty! before the Lord, in this particular. Let these now confess and bewail their own sin in the sight of God; and it was said in *Hos.* 14. 8. *What have I any more to do with Idols?* Thus let them say, *What have I any more to do with Devils?* The things that you have done, have been payments of Respects unto Devils; and it becomes you to *abhor your selves in dust and ashes* for your Folly. The great and terrible God says of you, as in *Deut.* 32. 21. *They have provocked me to anger with their Vanities.* Let the things that did provock him to anger, now provock you to sorrow. Retire this evening, and humble your selves very deeply, in that you have been so foolish and unwise. Lament all your Acquaintance with Hell; and let your Acquaintance with God be more. Let your Lamentations be more than ever your Divinations were.

Let them that have been guilty of Explicit Witchcraft, now also repent of their monstruous and horrid evil in it. If any of you have (I hope none of you have) made an express Contract with Devils, know that your promise is better broke than kept; it concerns you that you turn immediatly from the *Power of Satan unto God.* Albeit your sin be beyond all Expression or Conception heinous, yet it is not unpardonable. We read of *Manasseh* in 2 *Chron.* 33. 6. *He used Enchantments, and used Witchcraft, and dealt with a Familiar Spirit*

Spirit, and wrought much Evil in the sight of the Lord. But that great Wizzard found Mercy with God, upon his deep Humiliation for it: Such a boundless thing is the Grace of our God! the Prey of Devils, may become the Joy of Angels: The Confederats of Hell, may become the Inhabitants of Heaven, upon their sincere turning unto God. A Witch may be penitent in this, and glorious in another World. There was one *Hartford* here, who did with much Brokenness of Heart owne her Witchcraft, and leave her Master, and expire depending on the free Grace of God in Christ, and on that word of his, *Come to me, ye that labour and are heavy laden, and I will give you rest*; and on that, *There is a fountain open for sin and for uncleanness.* Come then, Renunce the Slavery and Interest of the Devils, Renunce your mad League with them. Come and give up your selves unto the Lord Jesus Christ, loathing your selves exceedingly for your so siding with the black enemies of his Throne. O come away from the doleful estate you are in. Come away from serving of the Devils that have ensnared your Souls. What wages have you from those Hellish Task-masters? Alas you are here among the poor, and vile, and ragged Beggers upon Earth. When did Witchcraft ever make any person rich? And hereafter you must be Objects for the intolerable Insolence and Cruelty of those Cannibals, and *be broken sore in the place of Dragons for evermore.* Betake your selves then to instant and constant Prayer, and unto your old filthy Rulers now say, *Depart from me, ye Evil Spirits, for I will keep the Commandments of God.* But we must now conclude with the Use of the third Proposition.

And that may be a Caution to every one of us. This in short, Since Rebellion is like Witchraft,

O let us not make light of any Rebellion against the Almighty GOD. Particularly,

First, Let not a Course of Rebellion be followed by us. It is the Course of unregenerat men to be dayly doing those things, for which *the wrath of God comes upon the children of disobedience.* When God requires, *Repent of Sin*, they do rebel and reply, *No, I have loved Idols, and after them I will go.* When God requires, *Believe on Christ*, they do rebel and reply, *No, I will not have this man to reign over me.* They rebel against all the Divine Commands of Love to God, or Love to Man. They rebel against all the Precepts of the Lord, which are to be esteemed concerning all things to be right. And they love every false way. O consider of this, ye strangers to the new Birth; Consider what you are doing, consider where you are going every day. I would now say, alluding to that in Dan. 4. 27. *O soul, let my counsel be acceptable unto thee, and break off thy sins.* You have been doing of Iniquity; O now say, *I will do so no more.*

Consider, First, There is a sort of Witchcraft charg'd on you. You shall as undoudtedly perish as any Witch in the world, except you reform. Can you imagine that an obstinat Witch will have Admission into the Kingdom of God? Behold, and be astonish'd, ye unrenewed ones; as impossible it is for you to see the Lord. It is said in Joh. 3. 2. *Verily, verily, I say unto thee, except a man be born again, he cannot see the kingdom of God.* That *verily verily*, which like a *flaming Sword*, stands to keep the vilest Witches out of Paradise, the same there is to keep every unbeliever out. The Lord said unto some confident pretenders of old, *Ye are as* Æthiopians *unto me.* This doth God say unto all them that obey him not; this doth he say to every one of you that do not fear him and keep his Commandments; he saith, *Ye are as Witches unto me*; though thy Birth be of goodly or gentile Parents, tho' thy Parts and Gifts may be extraordinary, tho thy Prayers may be twice a Week, and thy Alms enough to fill a Trumpet, yet become a new creature; otherwise *ye are as Witches unto me, saith the Lord.*

Consider, Secondly, There is a sort of Witchcraft come on you too. All that leave the way everlasting, and

tak

ake a way of wickedness, they are bewitched; a grievous Witchcraft has seiz'd upon them. The Apostle said to some in *Gal.* 3. 1. *O foolish Galatians, who hath bewitched you, that you should not obey the Truth?* This may be an Expostulation us'd with all ungodly men; *O foolish Transgressors, who has bewitched you?* I'le tell you who: Not an Hag, but a Lust has bewitched them. They that are bewitched, have a marvellous variety of calamity upon them. One while they can't see; that is thy case; Thou art wretched, but thou canst not see it; Christ is lovely, but thou canst not see him. One while they cannot hear; that is thy case; God calls, *Look unto me and be saved*; but thou hearest nothing of it. Another while they can't stirr; that is thy case; The Lord Jesus calls, *Come unto me*, but thou movest not. Sometimes they are as it were, cut and prickt, and distorted in their Limbs; the very same art thou in all the Faculties of thy soul. At other times they are pulled into the Fire, or into the Water, or thrown with violence upon the Ground; the like happens to thy unhappy soul; it is hurried thither, where the *fire is not quenched*; it is hurried thither where they *groan under the waters*; it is also made to *pant after the dust of the earth*. The drunken man is bewitched with strong drink; the unclean man is bewitcht with strange Flesh; the tongue of a Swearer is acted worse than the tongue of a bewitcht man; the covetous man is hideously bewitcht with Bags and Lands.

O pity thine own soul; and *give no sleep to thine eyes, nor slumber to thine eye-lids*, until thine immortal soul be deliver'd from thy natural state. Let not Witchcraft it self be a more frightful thing to thee, than thy own present Unregeneracy. *Turn ye, turn ye, why will ye die?*

Secondly, Let not an Act of Rebellion be allowed by us. When *Joseph* was incited unto an Ill Act, he said, in *Gen.* 39. 9. *How shall I do this wickedness, and sin against God?* Thus, when we are urged unto any ill Act, Let us refuse it so, *No, this is like Witchcraft, shall*

shall I by such Wickedness make my self as a Witch befor the Lord?

Three things are be Recommended here:

First, Arm your selves against all the Devices, wit which the Devils would hook you into any Rebellio against the Lord. For Rebellion against God, ther will be that clause in our Indictment, *They were mo ved by the Instigation of the Devil.* Now furnish you selves with Armour to keep off the Dint of the Devil Instigations; in short, *put on the whole Armour of God* There is specially a double Care that will be of grea use in your Encounters.

First, Use your Watch well. We read in *Eph.* 6. 11 about the Wiles of the Devil. When the Devil woul engage us in a Rebellion, there are certain wily Me thods by which he doth accomplish it. He work more by Fraud than by Force; and there is a cryptic method by which he doth gain us over to himself. A crafty Sophister has a three-fold Method with whic he prevails upon his Auditors; and such the Method o the Devil is. Watch, first, against the deficient me thod of the Devil. The Devil will show us the Si without the Curse, the Bait without the Hook: So h says *Eat the pleasant Fruit*; but he says not, *Thou shal die if thou do it.* The Devil will represent unto us th difficulty of a Duty, but conceal the recompence of it So he says, *It's a hard thing to pray in secret every day* but he says not, *Thy Father will reward thee.* And h will represent unto us the Excuse of a Sin, but co ceal the ill Shape of it: So he says, *Many others ha done this and that*; but he says not, *God was provock at it.* These are Tricks to be watched against.

Watch, secondly, against the Redundant Method the Devil. Sometimes the Devil will use a Digressio He will seem to give over his Intent in one thing, b make sure of his Intent in another. Such a Stratage he uses as what *Joshua* took *Ai* withal; he retires, an so he conquers. He will make Haughtiness and Secur ly undo the soul, that he could not make of his party for *grosser wickedness*. Sometimes the devil will use a *commoration*. He will dog a man, and bring Perswasion upon perswasion, as *Delilah* did with *Sampson*; and like a cunning *Fencer*, he *repeats* blow after blow, till he smite home. These are Dangers to be *watched* against.

Watch, Thirdly, against the *Inverting* Method of the Devil. One while the Devil will endeavour to carry us on from *Lesser* sins to *Greater* sins. He will go to make our miscarriages like *Elijah*'s cloud; at first as an *Handsbreadth*, but anon so as to hide the whole *Heaven* from us. So *Solomon* multiplies first *Horses*, and afterward *worse* things against the command of God. Another while, the Devil will decoy us from *lawful* things to *unlawful* things. Thus from a *Good husband*, a man shal grow a meer *Muck-worm*. Now and then also, the Devil will try to spoil Good works with Ill ends: Thus the Pride of *Jehu* shal be swell'd by the Zeal of *Jehu*. He will try to make our Duties Interfere; the general Calling shal be regarded in the season of the particular, and the particular Calling shal be attended with the season of the general. He will try to lead us from one Extream to another; We shal be excessively Merry, and ere long excessively Melancholly, if we hearken to him. O keep up your Watch. Well did the Apostle say, in 1. *Pet.* 5. 8. Be vigilant, *for the* Devil *as a roaring lion, seeketh whom he may devour*.

Secondly, Use your Sword well. This said in *Eph.* 6. 17. *Take the* Sword *of the Spirit which is the* Word *of God*. The Devil cannot stand before the *Brandishings* of this *two edged Sword*. Our Saviour overcame the devil by making that Return, *It is written*, and *It is written*, against all his lewd attempts. Would he get you into any Rebellion? One *Text* well managed will make him fly before you. Would he have you be Unjust? Then answer, It is written, *The unrighteous shall not inherit the kingdom of God*. Would he have you be Unclear? Then answer, It is written, *God reserves to be punished, them that walk in uncleanness.* Would he have you be immoderately Careful? Say then, It is written, *Cast thy burden on the Lord.*

This *Warefare* is directly contrary to that *Witchcraft* which the Devils are daily driving or drawing us unto.

Secondly, Beware of that Rebellion against God particularly, which the Devils are most gratified withal. It is said in *Eph* 4. 40. *Grieve not the holy Spirit of God.* The Unclean Devils are pleased most with such things as that Holy Spirit is most grieved with. Sometimes the Devils has been forced as it were, to discover their own Inclinations; through the mouths of Possessed persons they have declar'd what was very grateful to them. The Children that have been lately under a *diabolical Fascination* in this Town, have given us diverse Intimations, which we might make useful Observations on. I observed, that though they had much delight in Prayer when they were Well; yet when they were Ill, they could not endure it. The *Dæmons* would make them sing, and roar, and stop their ears, and plague them, and at last lay them for Dead, if any Prayer were in the Room. Whence it may be inferred, That you who can go without Prayer from day to day, do just as the Devils would have you. The Devils have an horrible Rendezvous in that Family, in that Closet, where Prayer is not maintained. I observed, that though the Word of God were their Companion and Counsellor at other times, yet now they would fall into *Convulsions*, if one did but look into a BIBLE. Whence it may be suppos'd that you who Read not the Scripture, for the most part every day, do humour the Devils in it. The Devils are glad to see the *Bibles* that have Dust upon them. I observed, that Hæretical, or Superstitious, or Profane Books, might be perused by some of them, when serious and Orthodox Books would put out their Eyes. Whence it may be suggested, That you who converse much with Ill Books, do as the Devils would: The Devils would willingly be where Jest=books, and Play-books, and Romances, and Hæresies

Hæresies or Supestitions are made a Library. I observed, that tho they were exemplary for Honesty and Sobriety, yet now their Wishes to Steal and be Drunk, were frequently expressed; and sometimes they were made very Drunk though no intoxicating Drink had been in the least an occasion of it. Whence it may be gathered, That the Drunkard has a Devil in him, the Stealer has a Devil in him. The Devils have sport enough, when they see a man Reeling in the streets; the Devils are the Comrades of them that go to Take what is none of their own. I observed, That though few in the place were so Diligent as they, nevertheless in their Fits they might not do any Work at all. Whence it may be concluded, That of Idleness comes no goodness. The Devils are the Play-mates of them that are Gaming when they should be Working. An Idle person is a Prentice of a Devil. These things have been Observed; and now let these Vices be Avoided. There is *Witchcraft* in them.

O that the Devils might be Out-shot in their own Bow, and that these Vices might be made Odious by their Affection for them.

Thirdly, Instead of Rebellion against God, let Obedience to God fill your lives. Make unto God that vow in *Psal.* 116. 16. *O Lord, truely I am thy servant*, &c. And accordingly, *serve God with all obedience.* Yea, *often* ask your selves, *What service may I do for God?* And let a respect of Obedience to God make even the Meanest of your Actions Honourable: even when you Eat and Drink, and Trade, and Visit, and Recreate your selves, let there be some Obedience to God in it all. The Employments of a poor Carpenter or Shooemaker will hereby be rendered more Noble things than the Victories of an *Alexander* or a *Cæsar*. Not the Devils but the Angels will have a most intimate Fellowship with a man thus Obedient: Not Witchcraft, but rather Inspiration will be in the Man who does this, and the Son of Man who layeth hold on it.

NOTAN-

Since the Finishing of the *History* which concerns *Goodwin's* Children, there has been a very wonderful Attempt made (probably by *witchcraft*, on another Family in the *Town*.) There is a poor Boy at this time under very terrible and amazing Circumstances, which a *Repetition* of, with not much *Variation* from those of the Children formerly Molested. The Person under vehement Suspition to be the Authors of this *Boy's* Calamities, is one that was complain'd of by those Children in their Ails. And accordingly one or two of those Children has at this time some Renewal of their Afflictions also; which perhaps may be permitted by the Great God, not to dissapoint our Expectations of their *Deliverance*, but for the *Detection* and the *Destruction* of more belonging to that hellish Knot, that has not yet perished as others of the Crew has done, before the poor Prayers of them that *Hope in* GOD.

The *Book*-sellers not being willing to stay the *Event* of these New Accidents, cause the *Bridles* here be taken off.

Appendix

THere are one or two Passages in the first of our foregoing Histories, which I foresee (those usually no less Absurd than angry People) the *Quakers*, will *come upon me with great wrath*, for my writing of: and the Incivilities lately shown to my Father, for a piece of one Chapter in his Book of *Remarkable Providences*, by one *Keith*, in a sort of a thing newly published at *Pensilvania*, have made it necessary for me, not only to explain my self, but to defend him, upon the occasion that is now before me.

As for what I have related concerning the strange liberty which the *Devils* gave unto *John Goodwin*'s Children, to enjoy both the *Writings*, and the *Meetings* of the *Quakers*, when offers thereof were (it may be too needlessly) made unto them. I need only acquaint the VVorld, that I shall produce good, legal, and sufficient Evidence to Confirm what I do Affirm, whenever any man shall demand it of me: And that the Books with which the Tryal happened to be made, were more than one, and such, as the *Quakers* give as general an Allowance to, as to their own *Primers* and their *Catechisms*. But undoubtedly, the matchless Candour and Sweetness of the *Quakers* will inspire them, with inclinations to give me some of their publick Thanks for the notice I have taken of them; and in the mean time I must let my Neighbours understand, what ridiculous, as well as odious Calumnies, the *Quakers* have bestowed upon my absent Father, for his being an Historian (they think) unto their prejudice.

One wou'd think, That if an Historian did but secure his *Veracity* from being Impeached, most of his other Faults were pardonable; and so truly they would be accounted by any, besides *Quakers*, who are a people *by themselves*. But my Father had published a Book, entituled *Illustrious Providences*; in one part of which, he has a Narrative of several very marvellous Occurrences, that certain deluded and possessed *Quakers*, in

this

this Countrey were concerned in: The Matter of Fact never could be disputed; yet one *Keith* a Quaker who had been compassing Sea and Land to make Proselytes, visits *New-Eng.* in his Progress, where meeting with small Applause, and less Success, in stead of Converts, he picks up what Quarrels our Countrey could afford him, and among the rest, this Book of *Providences.* At his Return to *Pensilvania,* he blesses the *VVorld* with a little Volumn of Heresies and Blasphemies against the Protestant Religion, the principle Articles whereof, he endeavours to undermine, with some further Improvements of Nonsense, than the Abilities of the *Quakers* had heretofore helped them to: but, though 'tis almost pity, that any Eagle (pardon the Comparison. he himself calls us *Night birds*) should lose his time, by attending the Motions of such a Fly; yet I suppose, he will not be long without the Castigations of a full, though short Answer, to the Impertinencies with which he has been craftily Assaying to spoil our Vines. He entitles his Harrangues, *The Churches in* New-England *brought to the Test*; and it might be expected, that one so willing to be a Servant of those Churches as *Increase Mather,* would not escape the Vengeance of those, whom these Churches are an Eye-sore unto. Accordingly, the Title Page of his Discourses, (for truly Reader, he will not now give us a *Silent Meeting*) promises to us, *An Answer to the gross Abuses, Lyes, and Slanders of* Increase Mather, which he afterwards detects, just as one of his Predecessors, after a Conversation with *Howsheads,* Trampled upon *Plato's* pride; while he cannot Instance in any one Abuse, Lye, or Slander of *Increase Mather,* without committing more than a few himself. However, he is pleas'd to say, when he comes to talk, Let any of his Kindred answer for him in his absence; and because I am somewhat a Kin to the said *Increase Mather,* whom the Animadversions of this *Keith,* have made such an Assault upon, that were I more dumb than the Son of *Croesus*

himself,

himself, yet I must have spoken at the Provocation, I am willing to satisfie our little Authour so far, as to Answer these three things upon him: Yet I would so far observe one of *Solomon*'s Rules in my Answer, as not to use upon him some Terms of his Art, which as a *Specimen* of his Breeding, he bestows upon *Increase Mather*; but offer a few just Reflections on this New Apostle (no doubt a Successor to one of the old ones) unto the World.

First, He charges my absent Father with gross Abuses, Lyes, and Slanders; and yet he denies not the Truth of the Stories, the Relation of which, flings him into this foaming Rage. He charges him, just as last year he did the rest of the Ministers of *Boston*. He sent us a written Challenge, which begins, *I being well assured by the Spirit of God, that the Doctrine ye preach to the People is false* ——— and he then reckons up Twelve Articles (he says) of our Doctrine, the Twelfth of which, is directly contrary to what we Assert, and Maintain and Preach every day. This was his Inspiration then! And such is his Narration now. *Increase Mather* Penns Truths, and yet it seems writes Lyes. But where is *Increase Mather*'s Crime? Why, our Animadvertor tells us, *J. M relates these Stories, on purpose to Abuse the honest and sober people called* Quakers, *without making any distinction* ——— But what Mettal is this Man's forehead made of? Reader, you shall find my Fathers Introduction to his Histories to be, *All wise men that are acquainted therewith, observe the blasting rebukes of Heaven upon the late Singing and Dancing* Quakers. And his inference from them is, That *the Quakers are some of them undoubtedly possessed with evil Spirits*; and his Conclusion is, *We may by this, judge whose servants the singing* Quakers *are*. Behold how carefully he has Repeated the very Distinction, which this waspish man complains at the Omission of! Besides, he had no need of making any Distinction at all. That the Quakers

Quakers fall out among themselves, is but a natura Consequence of their Tempers and Errors, which canno be otherwise than incoherent; and sometimes thei Credit forces them to Explode in one another, wha they (wish they could but) cannot Excuse. Thougl it seems if a Wo an dress her self like a Devil, and frigh some of her Sex almost out of their Lives on a Lord Day, in one of our biggest Assemblies, *G. K.* can her canonize her for a Saint. *Case*'s Crew are substantiall of the same Drove wi h *Keith*'s Crew; both Mad, thougl with some variety of Application in their Phrensies What if those Ranters, and these *Quakers* be shaken to gether in a Bag? 'Tis a more allowable Method of tort ing, that of this G. K.'s, who would make us a Cre of Ranters, because we hold, *That God hat foreordained infallibly, and unchangeably, whateve comes to pass.* And whereas our Answerer tell us, that when those horrid Monsters wer whipt at *Plimouth*, for their wonderful hideous Devilism *Some of the honest people called* Quakers, *openly declared befor the people, that the* Quakers *did not at all own them to b of their Society.* I am to ask him, who of this honest Peo ple then it was, That then declared them to be *the dea Children of God*? But Reader, pray observe, Though h will not leave Urging, that for a *Quaker* to be possessed is no more than for a *Presbyterian* or *Independent* so to be There is difference enough, where our notable Dispu tant could contrive a Parallel; because a Possession b evil Spirits, may befal one of our Communion. Wha then? The Possession does not move any to be of tha Communion: we see the contrary. But the Stories Re corded by my Father (plainly enough) demonstrat that Diabolical possession, was the thing which di dispose and encline men unto Quakerism; their Qua ke ism was the proper effect of the Possession; and no an unconcerned Consequent. 'Tis our Logicians Faul here, that he cavils without making any Distinction if he would have pleased to distinguish a little, he might have spared the pains of his tedious Excursions, about charging the innocent with the Crimes of the guilty. But from such a *G. K.* what better dealing might have been look'd for?

Secondly, I think, I may rather charge this *G. K.* with gross Abuses, Lies and Slanders, by him offer'd unto that *Increase Mather* whom he shows himself so much (beyond the cure of *Hellebore*) enflamed at. *He says*, Increase Mather *hath shew'd his Rashness and Folly in some other Passages of his Life, if not Malice, that hath occasion'd him for some time abscond, and depart from the place where he preached at* Boston. I am sorry that this man obliges me to trouble the World with Stories about such Domestick and Personal Matters as these are. For me to Commend my yet living Father, would perhaps be counted an Indecency. But if I should not now Defend him from such unhandsome Imputations, I were worse than the worst of the Sons of *Noah*, and it must be a greater Malice than what *G. K.* ever pretended to discover in *Increase Mather*, that shall Criminate my Vindication of an absent and a wronged Parent. My Readers Patience must then permit me to tell him, that all *New-England* well knows, That *Increase Mather* never departed from hence, through any Rashness or Folly of his own, but through the Malice of unreasonable men. Our Charter being unjustly Vacated (which even *G. K.* reckons among the Judgments of God upon us) the Government of this Territory was fallen into the hands of men that immediatly took all sorts of measures to make us miserable. A knot of people, that had no design but to enrich themselves on the ruines of this flourishing Plantation, were placed over us, and our Land Strangers devoured in our presence. The sight of our Calamities made my Father willing to undertake a Voyage unto *England*, for no other cause but meerly to endeavour the Service of his afflicted Countrey; and not a few among the principal Gentlemen of the place, did both Advise and Assist his Undertaking. His Intent-in going he did not publish, but his Intent of Going he did; and he had no sooner done it, but one *Randolph*, the late Secretary, whom (like a Scavenger) our late Oppressors chiefly used in their more dirty Businesses, gave Trouble unto him to obstruct and prevent his Voyage. The Circumstances of it were these: This *Randolph* some time since, carried unto Sir *Lionel Jenkins*, a Letter which he assur'd him was Mr. *Mather*'s; Though the Letter was a most Villanous Forgery, filled with Treason and Madness in the Exaltation of it, and never was one line of it written by my Father. The Letter-Forger had so foolishly drawn it up, That *Randolph* could not get the Blood of the Gentleman, whom he (after his manner, that is) falsly charged with being the Author of it, yet care was taken thereby to blast his Name: The Observator, (whom one calls the Father of Lies) here became Nurse, and Printed it, with not a few scurrilous Observations on it. So that in all the Taverns and Coffee-houses throughout three Kingdoms, this innocent Person was made a Ridicule, and *Barbados* too, with other of the Lee-ward Islands, took this opportunity to spit their Venom on one who had never done any thing to deserve it, but by being (in the account of some that are both) somewhat of a Learned and Honest man. My Father to Vindicat himself, while our old Government yet lasted, wrote a Letter to Mr. *Dudley*, who had from *White-Hall*, Received a Copy of that bloody Forgery; and in this Vindication, he intimats that several shrewd things would make him suspect *Randolph* himself to be the Director of it. It was evident unto him, That the whole Forgery was contrived for *Randolph*'s advantage; 'tis almost all of him and for him; but could any rational man imagine, that he was then wholly a Stranger to it? Beside there were in it several other Expressions, which ('twas then thought) no man in his Wits can dream that any without him should have. But *Randolph* upon his Arrival here with our New Government getting a Copy of my Fathers Vindication, does after so many months [illegible] him in an *Action of Defamation*, to Embarass the Affairs he had before him. The Jury which consisted partly of Church of *E.* [illegible] men, Found for my Father against the Plaintiffe. And yet just within a Week or two before his Voyage, *Randolph* renewed his Action; his Abetters resolving (as I am credibly informed) That having laid the Arrest upon him, they would have secur'd his person in the Goal, as the worst of Traitors; for what *Illegality* would they stick at? He happily understanding, what they would be at, by the counsel of his Friends withdrew, for about a Week, and then, tho' both by Day and Night, both by Land and Sea, the late Spirits among us way laid him, God carried him safely thro them all; and when he came to *Witchall* what Favours the Greatest Men in the Kingdom have heap'd upon him, 'tis not Proper for me to tell. Whereas our Caviller now says, *It wants to be insert in his Book, that what hath befallen him of late, is a Remarkable Judgment of God upon him, for his Injustice to the Quakers.* I join issue with him, and beg the Reader to insert it, if he be owner of that harmless Book. Reader, inasmuch as none of *Increase Mathers* enemies were able to attain their ends upon him; and inasmuch as this *Increase Mather* has in his whole Negotiation for *New-England*, been favoured by the merciful God, beyond the imagination of our fondest hopes; pray count it, *A Remarkable Judgment of God upon him, for his Injustice to the Quakers.* This *G. K.* has this Book of his bound up in Canvas, because I suppose, like one of the Witnesses, he would Prophesie in Sackcloth. I confess, *Fire proceeds out of his mouth*; but it is another sort of Fire than that which our Lords Witnesses are us'd unto; and there is one small Qualification of a Witness which you see he wants, that is, Truth; the Contents of his Books requires some other Covers for them, *ne perpluat*.

Thirdly, Not *Increase Mather* alone, but all *New-England*, especially the Shepherds of the Churches here, must through the Lycanthropy of this man, be Barked at. One while his false Histories misrepresent us to the World, and he raises dismal Tragedies upon the Persecution which his Friends here have met withal. For my own part, I have long wished, That the Civil Magistrat would never inflict a Civil Penalty, on an Heretick; until Humane Society receive such a Disturbance from him, as in one or mine, or any other perswasion were intollerable. Yet there is more, far more to be said for the Justification of our ancient Severities on two or three Quakers here, than the World has yet been acquainted with. *Oliver Cromwel* himself, whose Toleration of Sectaries was notorious enough, yet would speak in the Justification of what was here done to them. Since our *Jerusalem* was come to such a Consistence, that the *going up of every Fox would not break down our stone wall*, who ever medled with them? And since that, Though a Quaker-woman came (as sometimes they have) stark naked, into some of our Solemn Assemblies, declaring her self to be a Sign; yet the Bruit has not been thought fit to be Hang'd up: but the Generality of the people are enough, and always were, averse to the inflicting of Secular Punishments on these doting Hereticks. Indeed a Grave Magistrat once ('tis said) propounded unto the General Court at *Plimouth*, a Law a Law that every *Quaker might have his head shaved*; because they were distracted, and this would both shame and cure them. I believe this is all the Law that ever will be offered for the Suppressing of them here; by long experience, we find, *They perish by being let alone.* But whereas he twits the Ministers here, for their Accepting of Maintainance, with *goods unjustly taken from the true owners*; I may inform the World, the Ministers here are of another Spirit than so; their voluntary Poverty and transcendent Self-Denial, has scarce its parallel in the Christian World. If any Maintainance extorted from Quakers hath ever been paid unto them, I am confident it was without their knowledge or consent. The chief Complaints of this kind are in *Plimouth* Colony; but let the Reader consider, That the Grants of Lands there made by the Court, have still been with an Express Condition and *Proviso*, that the allowed Ministry be therewith supported. Quakers come and Accept and Improve these Grants, and then refuse the Duty annexed thereunto. Let all mankind judge whether they might not justly be compell'd unto the payment of it? yet how rarely was it ever done? *G. K's. Barnstable* Story is (I hear) a Romance of the same piece with the rest. But we must be terrified with his false Prophecies too. He pretends to Inspiration and foretells *the utter Removing, Undoing, and Destroying of all our Babylonish Buildings*, that is, our Churches: and he adds, *The time hastens, and blessed shall be he who receiveth the Warning*; and some Pages after he predicts, that *In due time our Meeting-Houses shall no more receive us into them.* Ay, no doubt of it, *in due time*! But, I pray Friend *George*, when is this due time to be? Our late Persecutors, who did last year admit thee to so much familiarity with them, did not so wisely to let thee know what they were driving at, for it seems thou art a Blab of thy tongue. When thy privat Conversation with them, as vvell as their publick Administration here, gave thee cause to guess, That our Churches vvere quickly to be overturned, and our Meeting-Houses made too hot for us, 'tvvas easie to Prognosticat much more than this; I'le assure thee, 'tvvas not for this that I put thee into my Book of Witchcrafts, there vvas no Witchcraft in it: but some late things have a little altered our *Omens*. I humbly beg of God, that he vvould *requite us good for this Cursing this day*; and that the malicious Vaticinations of men that hate the Truth and Ways, may rather help to procure for us those happy Revolutions, which may cause our enemies to be [illegible]. [illegible] also entreat the Reader that he would not mis-interpret my approaches (if I have made any) towards Levity in my Treating of the *Adversary standing at my Fathers right hand to resist him*; 'Tis almost impossible to look upon the Generality of Quakers, without applying to them the Humour which a Gentleman long since thought [illegible] contrived on purpose, to be made merry with. I shall only add, That *George Keith* has given sufficient cause why his own Sect should be ashamed of him, if Shame were compatible to such a perfect People. But as he thinks my Father wants *The true eye opened in him*, so I suppose he will tell me, *That I am in the dark*; and therefore it is time for me to bid him now *Good-Night.* I am not willing to contend any further with him, For

> *Hac scio pro certo, quando cum stercore certo*
> *Vinco, seu vincor, semper ego maculor.*

FINIS.

CPSIA information can be obtained
at www.ICGtesting.com
Printed in the USA
BVHW051206070221
599586BV00020B/815